NANTUCKET STYLE

I live on an island at sea
And that is just great for me,
There is swimming and fishing
And roses and birds,
And the wind is so gentle and free

Angela Allen
grade 3
Nantucket Elementary School
1980

First published in the United States of America in 1990 by
RIZZOLI INTERNATIONAL PUBLICATIONS, INC.
300 Park Avenue South, New York, NY 10010

Library of Congress Cataloging-in-Publication Data

Linsley, Leslie.
    Nantucket style / Leslie Linsley ; photographs by Jon Aron.
      p.   cm.
    ISBN 0-8478-1165-4
    1. Architecture, Domestic—Massachusetts—Nantucket Island.
  2. Decorative arts—Massachusetts—Nantucket Island.   3. Nantucket
  Island (Mass.)—Social life and customs.   I. Aron, Jon.   II. Title.
  NA7235.M42N365   1990
  728′.37′0974497—dc20   89-43255
                                                                CIP

Set in type by David E. Seham Associates, Metuchen, New Jersey
Map drawn by T.R. Lundquist
Printed and bound by Toppan Printing Company, Tokyo, Japan

NANTUCKET STYLE

LESLIE LINSLEY

PHOTOGRAPHY
JON ARON

DESIGN
SMATT FLORENCE INC

RIZZOLI
NEW YORK

CONTENTS

NANTUCKET ISLAND

NANTUCKET STYLE

While this book was a labor of love—love of a place and a love for those who make it special—it could not have happened without the help of so many people who were willing to give of their time, offer suggestions and encouragement, make introductions on our behalf, and open their homes to us. Making new friends as a result of this project was perhaps the greatest reward. Writing about and photographing a place with which we are so familiar made us rediscover the island. Through this rediscovery, we are more aware of the importance of the preservation of the island's natural beauty and historic architecture.

Living on a little patch of earth thirty miles from the mainland brings people together. There is a shared sense of pride for this place. When we were photographing an eighteenth-century house, its owner expressed a lovely sentiment about her home: "We are just caretakers . . . and responsible for appreciating what is here and respecting what was." This sums up how the residents of Nantucket feel about the island.

It is with respect and appreciation that we extend our thanks to those who have supported our efforts. We have produced many books together, but none has given us the sense of satisfaction we have derived from this project. For that opportunity, we very much want to thank our editor at Rizzoli, Robert Janjigian, who had the vision to take on this project and the patience and fortitude to keep it on track during a difficult schedule. We would also like to thank Karin Smatt and Michael Roberts of Smatt Florence Inc for a perceptive interpretation of our work. And we especially want to thank our agent, Berenice

Hoffman, who encouraged us to do this project in the first place.

Our appreciation goes out to Mimi Beman of Mitchell's Book Corner who encouraged us almost daily; to Julie Sanford, who has been a friend, liaison, and a great help (grasping the concept of the book from the beginning, her introductions made it possible to include some exceptional houses we might otherwise have missed); and to Robby Smith, who kept things running smoothly in the studio while we were on location. We are equally indebted to Gene Mahon and his able staff at The Camera Shop.

We are grateful to the following Nantucket people for their generous contributions to this book: Ethel and George Anastos; Gretchen Anderson; Ursula and Philip Austin; Jack Bangs and Michael Moliner of Flowers at The Boarding House; Bonnie and Elliott Barnett; Betsy Barvoets of the Artist's Association of Nantucket; Jinny and Joseph Beaulieu; Heidi L. and Max N. Berry; Noel Berry; Maddy and Bud Bohnsack; Anne and David Bradt; Paul Bruno; Judy and Charles Darby; Raymond Dawson, Jr.; Don DeMarco; Penny Dey; Charles W. Douglas, Jr.; Liza Dyche; Kitty Goldsmith; Grace and Bernard Grossman; Anne Grieves; Nina Hellman; Virginia and George J. Hill III; Arthur Hensler; Judith and Harold Heustein; Pamela and Reid Humphreys; Richard Kemble; Shelly and Thomas Kennelly; George Korn; Gary Knight; Reggie Levine; Carol and Karl Lindquist; Miriam and Seymour Mandell; Maggie Meredith; Carol and Robert Miller; Margaretta Grandin Nettles; Andy Oates and William Euler of Nantucket Looms; Karl and Susan Chase Ottison; June and Henry Pfeiffer; Francine and David Place; Susan and Frederick Ranney; Bonnie Ray; Nancy and Peter Rodts; Rose and Louis Rubin; Donn Russell; Ellen J. Selden; Arthur Schaefer; Avis Skinner; Dorothy and William L. Slover; Ann and Thomas Sollas, Jr.; Jane and Scott M. Stearns, Jr.; Frances and J. Gwynne Thorsen; Harry Wagtenveld of Grass Roots Bloomists; Carolyn and Robert Walsh; William Welsh; Elizabeth Winship; Mrs. Joseph C. Woodle; Livingston Wright, Jr.; and Cynthia Young.

Special thanks to Elizabeth Oldham, executive director of the Nantucket Island Chamber of Commerce, for information used in the source listings; The Nantucket Historical Association; and the Nantucket Conservation Foundation.

Leslie Linsley and Jon Aron
Nantucket, Massachusetts

Above: Hither Creek.
Left: A quiet field off Mill Street.
Overleaf: The Brant Point Lighthouse stands at the entrance to Nantucket harbor.

NANTUCKET ISLAND

INTRODUCTION

Left: A view of Nantucket town from the
tower of The First Congregational Church.
Above: Charming cottages line the wharves in
the marina.

Main Street, Nantucket Island.

Visitors to Nantucket travel by steamship from
the Massachusetts mainland.

Back in the 1930s, a group of my father's friends invited him to go on a fishing excursion to a place called

Nantucket Island. He had never heard of the place and his friends were only slightly more knowledgeable.

They weren't even sure exactly where it was, but, having mastered the Long Island Sound off the coast

of Connecticut, they were itching to take their boats into more adventuresome waters. On a map, Nan-

tucket must have looked like quite a spot on which to set their sights.

That trip made an indelible impression on my father. As the family story goes, by the time this young

lawyer brought his new wife to Nantucket Island several years later, he was convinced that he alone had

discovered this faraway isle. My mother must have been impressed. It was love at first sight. Years later,

having spent childhood summers on the island, I moved here as an adult. I, too, felt like it was "my island."

Actually, it was Captain Bartholomew Gosnold, an Englishman, who sailed to Nantucket in 1602 and put it on the map. In 1641, Thomas Mayhew purchased the island, and for the next two hundred years the island population grew and prospered into an established, self-contained community thirty miles off the coast of Massachusetts.

The history books tell it all: the hardships of the early settlers; the excitement in 1712 when the first spermaceti whale was caught (launching an industry that enabled this little community to prosper); the setbacks of two wars; and the resiliency of a determined population of less than five thousand that, by the 1830s, helped make Nantucket known throughout the world. No other community of this size has had such an impact on the world as this seven-by-thirteen-mile, isolated island. And the mere mention of its name evokes images of romance and mystery, a place to get away from the real world, a town that has been likened to Brigadoon.

But it wasn't always so, and perhaps this is Nantucket's greatest asset today. After fifteen years of prosperity from whaling, the islanders got to feeling pretty secure, thinking the boom times would last forever. Then, in 1846, two devastating events changed Nantucket. First, the discovery of petroleum put an end to the need for whale oil, and second, a major fire, thereafter known as The Great Fire of 1846, destroyed a third of the town. Many young people were forced to leave the island in order to make a living and real-estate values plummeted. Nantucket became like a ghost town

and would not make a comeback for almost fifty years, this time in the form of a summertime resort.

Combine the sorry shape of the island's economy after the fire with the drop in population and what you have is a town frozen in time for almost fifty years, untouched by the effects of the Industrial Revolution. As a result, Victorian architecture, so rampant on the mainland, generally bypassed Nantucket.

As early as 1870, when morale was at an all-time low and the town had not a ship to its name, some inventive people began designing promotion pieces to attract tourists to Nantucket. They expounded on the virtues of its sea air and healthy environment. "There is no malaria on Nantucket," was one such lure. Another, appealing to the imagination of the weekend fishermen, held out the promise of a successful day at sea. Indeed the idea must have caught on, for by 1872, the first "party boat," *Lizzie and Helen,* cruised around Nantucket for ten hours. Sixty bluefish were caught.

At the height of the whaling era,

Siasconset, the fishing village at the east end of the island, offered a restful haven for wealthy Nantucketers. It was not considered fashionable, but as a change from the ordinary, 'Sconset, as it is known, offered picturesque charm and a refreshing place to rest mind and body. When the town of Nantucket became popular as a summer resort, 'Sconset was discovered.

But it was the south shore of Surfside that Nantucket thought would hold the most attraction as a resort area. In 1881, three hundred descendants of Tristram Coffin, from all over the United States, gathered for a clambake at Surfside beach. (You can imagine such an event today. You couldn't keep the place a secret if you tried.) When they returned home, relatives and friends of relatives spread the word that Nantucket was the place to spend a vacation.

While Surfside never made it as a "town," 'Sconset was reconsidered and a railroad was built to carry vacationers out to the little village. It became a popular theatrical commu-

nity by the turn of the century, where famous actors could have a somewhat undisturbed respite and perform at the newly built 'Sconset Casino.

Almost a hundred years later, not much has changed here. The railroad has given way to a bicycle path, attracting health-conscious people, young and old alike, who find the invigorating fourteen-mile round-trip bike ride, with a tour of this fishing village at the end of the path, one of the best reasons to vacation here.

As a resort, Nantucket has surpassed the wildest dreams of those first visionaries. It has achieved a level of sophistication that comes from adapting to whatever is new and elegant while retaining an atmosphere of casual simplicity and its own traditions. For this reason it continues to attract celebrities and socialites. Private jets and yachts coming in and out of the little airport and harbor supply a bit of welcome glamour all summer long. But it is also accessible to the casual traveler. During the height of the sea-

son, the island swarms with tourists who come for a week or two or just for a day trip on the ferry from Hyannis. Everyone comes for the same reason: to experience the natural beauty and charm of this historic island.

Nantucket Island is located thirty miles off the coast of Cape Cod, Massachusetts, and can be reached in two and a half hours by boat or about an hour by plane from Boston or New York City. If you live in Texas or Washington, D.C., where many of Nantucket's summer residents reside in the winter, it can take a bit longer, given the fog and other weather conditions that regularly stop or delay service to the island. But once "America," as locals refer to the mainland, has been left behind, visitors to Nantucket agree that it's well worth the trouble.

Nantucket is more than a place—it's a state of mind. First-time visitors to the island are often struck by its physical quaintness and the charm and plainness of its Quaker-influenced buildings. Grey and weathered shingles, fences defining close-set yards, railed entrances, and twelve-over-twelve-paned windows typify island architecture. Everything is in harmony and of a piece, and this has a calming effect on the visitor who may have left a more hectic world behind. There are no commercial signs or traffic lights, no visual or noise pollution. And so far, fast-food chains haven't invaded the landscape, due to the determination of a watchful Historical Association. In fact, the undesirable architecture that one finds elsewhere is absent from Nantucket, accounting for much of its beauty.

Top left: The Unitarian-Universalist Church, built in 1809, is a Nantucket landmark. The church is known for its Lisbon bell, Goodrich organ (the oldest of its kind in its original setting), and a wonderful trompe l'oeil interior.
Bottom left: Union Street under a blanket of fresh-fallen snow.
Top center: Built in 1774, the Old North Wharf is one of Nantucket's oldest wharves.
Above: Swain's Mill, built in 1746 of timbers from wrecked ships, grinds corn to this day.
Below: A collection of colorful buoys decorates the side of a shed.

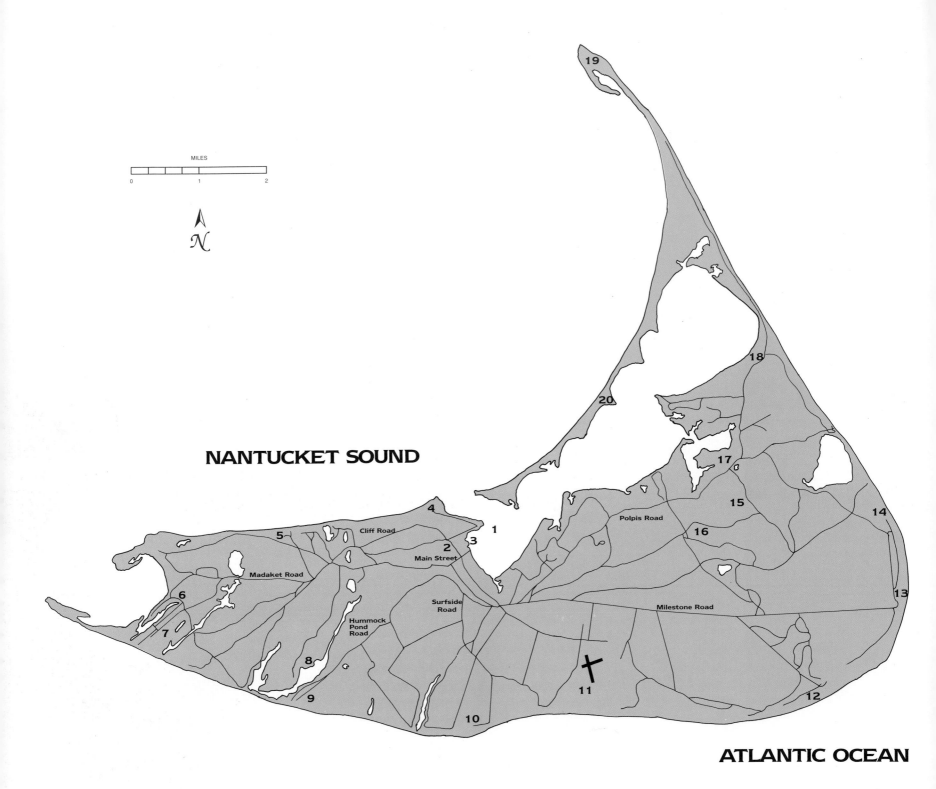

NANTUCKET SOUND

ATLANTIC OCEAN

MILES
0   1   2

N

19

18

20

17

15

14

Polpis Road

16

13

Milestone Road

4

Cliff Road

1

5

2

3

Main Street

Madaket Road

Surfside Road

6

Hummock Pond Road

7

8

11

9

10

12

ISLAND MAP

Nantucket Harbor in high season.

Yet, Nantucket is not a made-to-order town. It boasts a colorful history and is the way it is because it has evolved. It isn't surprising that changes of any sort were slower to catch on here than on the mainland; in particular, the way Nantucketers designed their houses. The architectural styles that were affecting the building trades elsewhere weren't catching on with islanders, not only because of the island's remote location, but, more profoundly, due to the strong Quaker influence of a more practical and simple way of life. Also, old Nantucket did not produce any architects of significant note, though there were many splendid craftsmen. Most of the houses in town were built by ship's carpenters familiar with balance and symmetry and they applied this knowledge to building houses.

The interiors of the well-preserved early homes (more than eight hundred houses built between 1740 and 1840 remain) reveal an efficiency of space, paneled walls, and flat, strong, simple trim associated with ship cabins—even doors with slant-ing tops that were commonplace on ships. The carpenters' handling of materials affected the design of mantels, doors, and windows. Indeed, these characteristics are influencing restoration efforts, and, in some instances, the building of new homes on the island today.

**Above, top: An early cemetery provides a fascinating glimpse into the history of the island.
Above: The flower and vegetable carts from Barlett's and Mt. Vernon farms pull in at opposite corners of Main and Federal Streets each morning.
Right: The sun sets behind The First Congregational Church at day's end.**

NATURAL
BEAUTY

Nantucket Island is a fragile piece of land. It is a remnant of an ancient coastline that was altered by glaciers centuries ago. Today, the island is a classic glacial moraine of ridge dropping to low hills and flat plains that lead to sandy beaches all around. The island is an ever-changing environment as the ocean forms and reforms its shape.

The moors on Nantucket, thought to be the most scenic area of the island, provide a network of paths to walk through. Similar to the Scottish heaths, this area is covered with low shrubs and wildflowers and hosts native deer and a variety of small animals and birds. At one time this area was called The Commons and was used for raising sheep. Over-grazing of the land led to its eventual return to the wild.

There are dozens of ponds on Nantucket. Some, like Sasachacha, Capaum, and Hummock ponds, are separated from the sea by a thin sandbar. There are many "kettle" ponds dotting the island, formed by huge chunks of ice left behind by the receding glacier. They seem to pop

Above, left: A large portion of Nantucket Island is preserved as a natural environment. These areas are posted with markers of the Nantucket Conservation Foundation.
Left: Winter at Madaket beach on the west end of the island.
Above: Long Pond, on the way to Madaket.
Right: A path to Jetties beach.

up in unexpected places, perhaps symbolic of their creation.

The shores of Nantucket are soft and vulnerable. Here, the sea does its work swiftly. Every summer, visitors are surprised to see that their favorite beaches have changed. Sometimes a beach may be reduced to the width of a roadway or it may have expanded to twice its former size. The beaches at Surfside, Nobadeer, Tom Nevers, 'Sconset, Quidnet, Squam, Wauwinet, Coatue, Jetties, Dionis, Madaket, and Cisco form a clean, white, soft border around this green island.

Left: Hither Creek.
Above: A walking path through the moors.
Above, right: Looking out toward the sea at Hummock Pond.
Near right: Looking out toward Nantucket Harbor in the fall.
Far right: Sunset at Madaket beach.

BEYOND THE FRONT DOOR

Left: One of the bedrooms in the 1724 Captain Richard Gardner house.
Above: Sunlight fills the hallway of 19 Lily Street.

This fine collection of maritime antiques includes early lightship baskets, unusual carved ivory pieces, and scrimshaw.

A guest bedroom tucked under the eaves of the original wing at 77 Main Street.

Though Nantucket is rooted in its unique history, it is really the relationship between its historic past and current influences that characterizes the island's appealing style—whether in interior design, arts and crafts, or gardens.

During the height of the island's prosperity, Nantucketers were coming into contact with people of diversified backgrounds. The sea may have isolated them in one regard, but it also provided a link to the world beyond, much the way our highways do today. It was by way of the sea that whalemen were exposed to Europe, Africa, and Asia. They were as familiar with the Orient as any port along the eastern seaboard, and their homes were often filled with treasures brought back from their seafaring travels.

Things aren't much different today. Nantucket homes are filled with beautiful objects, some from the

Left: A faux-finish floorcloth, painted by Dorothy Slover, decorates the front parlor of her home at 77 Main Street.
Right: The Quaker influence is seen in the elegantly simple dining room of the Grieves house on Mill Street.

island and many brought here from travels around the world. The islanders' love of decorating their homes is a passion that is as much a part of Nantucket style as creating a cottage garden or cooking a fine meal.

In fact, one of the first places Nantucket residents go when they arrive on island is Mitchell's Book Corner at the head of Main Street. Owner Mimi Beman is second-generation to the business, and knows just about everyone here. She says, "Style books are very popular with Nantucket home owners. The residents of Nantucket are quite passionate about their homes. Decorating is one of their favorite activities when they're here."

But designing island interiors is not a simple task. Island decorator Gary Knight often refers to the late Billy Baldwin when talking about decorating. Billy was a longtime summer resident of Nantucket and many of the houses here have remnants of his influence. "Begin by removing things," Gary paraphrases the famous decorator. Gary designs with

Nantucket in mind and is responsible for many of the interiors of some of the island's finer homes. "I strive to create a soothing environment," Gary continues. "There is so much natural beauty here on Nantucket— the moors, the ponds, the harbors, town—I really don't want my rooms to compete with what's going on outside. That doesn't mean I only do white rooms, but people come to Nantucket for its serenity and beauty and I think a house should reflect that."

One source for decorators and home owners alike is located on cobblestoned Main Street between Union and Washington Streets, The Nantucket Looms. Practically an institution on Nantucket, The Looms, as it is familiarly known, was founded by the Nantucket Historical Trust twenty-eight years ago with the help of its present owners, William Euler and Andy Oates. The shop is devoted to producing consistently high-quality, handwoven fabrics for clothing and home furnishings. One of the pleasures of selecting fabrics here is watching

the weaving process right in the store.

Besides being seen in numerous Nantucket homes, the handwoven fabrics can be found in the East Wing of the National Gallery in Washington, D.C., the gallery of the IBM executive building in New York City, and other corporate headquarters around the country.

Along with the handwoven fabrics, the shop carries a select group of exquisite gifts and accessories for the home, many by island craftworkers. The careers of many talented craftspeople have been launched because of this association. Liz Winship, manager of the shop, says, "We are always looking for that which is well-designed, beautifully made, and fairly priced. It's what the shop stands for and why Nantucketers come here."

Margaretta Nettles is one designer who acquired an international reputation through The Nantucket Looms. She is now the owner of The Weaving Studio on Union Street. Her tapestries grace many island homes where the owners are

concerned with quality. Her large, seamless, woven rugs are especially appreciated in some of the larger homes. Anna Lynn at The Weaving Room on Orange Street creates smaller area rugs. Home owners visiting the studio can help in the creative process of choosing their colors and materials.

When it comes to interiors, Avis Skinner, owner of Vis-a-Vis on Main Street, has a good eye for spotting just the right antique quilts, hooked rugs, and unusual accessories that belong in Nantucket homes. Her shop is the culmination of many years in business here, and she says the people who come here are often buying for their houses off island as well. "They find unusual items on Nantucket, the kinds of things they might not find elsewhere. Nantucket is unique that way. It's what keeps the island so special."

For home accessories and gifts, many islanders also turn to Liza Dyche, owner of Petticoat Row, an exquisite shop at 19 Centre Street. "Nantucket home owners appreciate items of quality, but definitely don't want anything pretentious," Liza says. "They're concerned with making their environments pretty as well as comfortable and tend to buy the finer things." She says that people are spending more time creating outdoor living areas. Her garden furniture is especially popular because it's beautifully designed and made with practical materials, an important consideration on this island of fickle weather.

It's no wonder Liza's garden furniture does a flourishing business. Gardening is more popular than ever. Everyone has or wants a gar-

Left: A mid-eighteenth-century French window treatment is employed in the living room of the Mandell's Union Street home.
Above: Floral prints and green plants, against a background of white, create a light and airy living room on Union Street. The angled ceilings and living spaces on different levels bring interest to this small house. French doors lead to a deck.

den, and it's contagious. No matter how small the yard, you'll find a Nantucket flower bed. Fences can barely contain the cosmos and daisies that strain to reach the sun, and no decent fence would be worth its pickets if it weren't laden with roses. From April right through Christmas, The Garden Center and Bartlett's Ocean View Farm are the busiest places on island.

As many Nantucket home owners are on island for only three or four days at a time, some satisfy their passion for flowers by calling Harry Wagtenveld of Grass Roots Bloomists at Zero Washington Street. With merely a phone call from his clients, Harry can have their rooms filled with flowers before they arrive.

"Most of my clients like a garden look," Harry explains. "There are so many beautiful wildflowers growing all over Nantucket, and people tend to extend this look into their homes It's less formal, looser, more like an English bouquet." Like Michael Molinar and Jack Bangs of Flowers at The Boarding House, Harry also creates arrangements that are "carefully casual."

Another influence on the interior style of Nantucket homes is a subculture of furniture exchange. Often, furnishings are recycled from one attic to another through yard sales, local auctions, and Attic Industries, a secondhand shop. It is not unusual to find pieces of furniture that once belonged to Billy Baldwin residing in various island homes, a result of the auctioning of his estate after his death. I consider my French cane dining chairs among my most cherished pieces because they were once in Billy's house.

What isn't bought at sales and secondhand shops can be found in the island's antique and folk art shops. Visitors to Nantucket find plenty here to satisfy the most discerning taste. The Chamber of Commerce lists no less than twenty-one antique shops in and around town. A tour through any Nantucket home will reveal an astonishing level of quality and style, especially in maritime artifacts.

Nina Hellman, whose shop on Broad Street specializes in scrimshaw and Nantucket memorabilia, says, "There are some serious collectors on Nantucket. They're knowledgeable about nautical antiques and they look for specific things to add to their collections. Others want one or two items, like a sailboat model or a piece of scrimshaw, to have in their Nantucket houses." Nina says old maps and early souvenirs, especially little watercolors of early Nantucket, are very much in demand. "People are crazy for maps and are fascinated with the physical changes that have occurred on the island," she adds.

Almost any house you happen into will have at least one or two unique artifacts that relate to Nantucket's history. And visitors to Nantucket never hesitate to take home a little bit of the island's past, whether a lightship basket, an old map, or a sailboat model, to enrich the spirit.

While historical artifacts continue to fascinate residents and visitors, local artists are having an impact on the island's galleries and serious collectors. Reggie Levine, owner of The Main Street Gallery, has lived on Nantucket all his life and owned the gallery for the past twenty

years. Scenes of Nantucket used to comprise the major portion of the gallery's sales, but this isn't so anymore. In fact, Reggie says that while he used to carry one hundred percent Nantucket artists, today the mix is half and half.

"The approach to buying art on Nantucket has changed a great deal since I first opened the gallery," he says. "Summer homes used to be far more casual, decorated with secondhand furniture, with a summery feeling. In the last fifteen years, homes have become more formal. People are entertaining more, so they want their homes to reflect their lifestyle. Some of the people who come here have two and three homes and they travel regularly to Europe. This has had an influence on their attitudes about buying art in general. When they come to Nantucket, they buy art for their summer homes in a more discerning way. They aren't just looking for something to hang over the sofa."

Reggie continues, "And for this reason some of the newer, very good island artists like George Murphy, Loretta Domaszewski, Sterling Mulbry and David Cross, to name a few, have been appreciated." Reggie adds that people want consistency in their style of living. They feel their island homes should be as comfortable and tastefully decorated as their off-island homes, and this means a serious attitude about the art they choose to live with.

A fascinating collection of coronation souvenir tins is displayed in a corner of artist Donn Russell's Nantucket dining room.

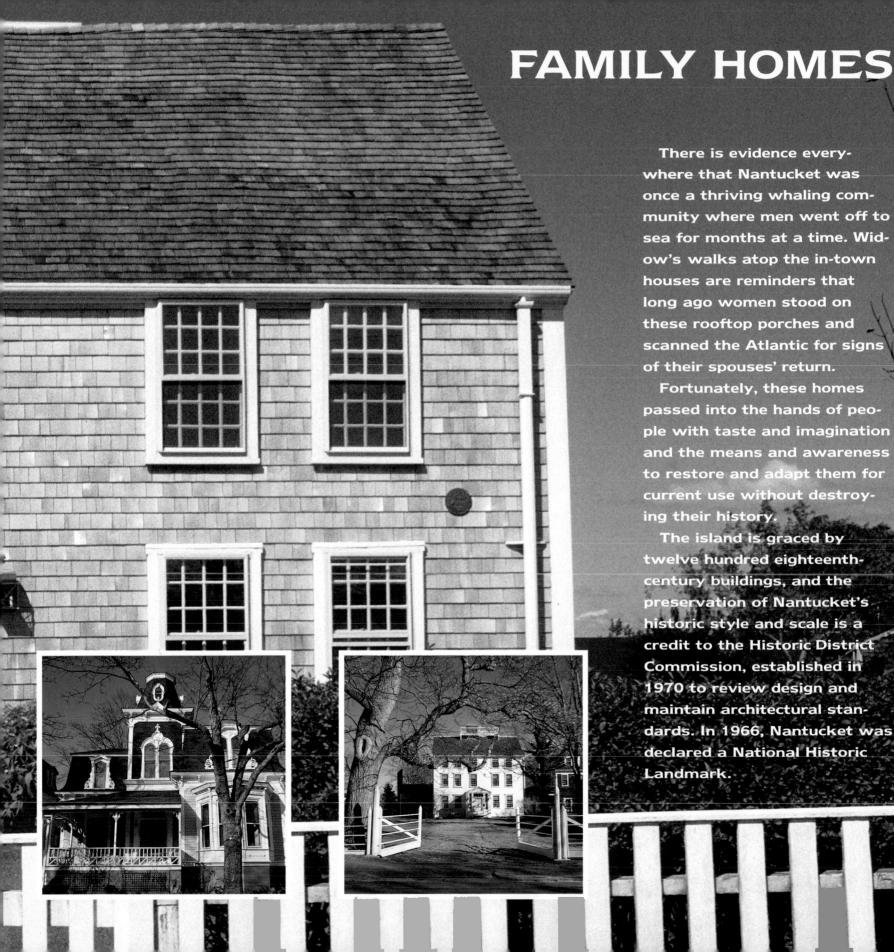

FAMILY HOMES

There is evidence everywhere that Nantucket was once a thriving whaling community where men went off to sea for months at a time. Widow's walks atop the in-town houses are reminders that long ago women stood on these rooftop porches and scanned the Atlantic for signs of their spouses' return.

Fortunately, these homes passed into the hands of people with taste and imagination and the means and awareness to restore and adapt them for current use without destroying their history.

The island is graced by twelve hundred eighteenth-century buildings, and the preservation of Nantucket's historic style and scale is a credit to the Historic District Commission, established in 1970 to review design and maintain architectural standards. In 1966, Nantucket was declared a National Historic Landmark.

GRACIOUS LIVING ON MAIN STREET

After recovering from the War of 1812, Nantucket prospered more than ever before. Whale oil was in demand, as were the byproducts of the whaling industry. There were seventy-two island-owned whalers and the population had swelled to seventy-three hundred, just about what it is today. Prosperity meant good jobs for everyone. For the first time, capitalism had come to Nantucket. By the turn of the century, more millionaires lived on Nantucket than anywhere else in the United States.

The influx of money led to the building of grander homes. But, since change came slowly to Nantucket, building was still done with a traditional sensibility. One of the major changes of the Federal period that followed the American Revolution was the removal of a central chimney, replaced by end chimneys so fireplaces could be located on the outside walls, with one in each room. Rooms became larger, staircases grander, and wider windows graced the facades. A front doorway with side windows was another break with tradition.

The large imposing house which stands at the corner of Main Street and Walnut Lane, just up from the Pacific National Bank, shows the dwindling influence of the Quakers and the increased financial status of the man who built it.

Built at the same time that Joseph Starbuck was building his famous Three Bricks (houses for his three sons just up the street), 77 Main Street is part of a building boom typifying a period of the greatest affluence on Nantucket. Considered together, these grand Main Street houses comprise the dominant style of building in the 1830s. Variations of this Neoclassical style can be seen all over the island today. Almost all of the reconstruction after the fire of 1846 followed the Greek-Revival style. There are almost two hundred examples remaining in Nantucket town.

Historians refer to 77 Main Street as the Francis Macy house (1790s). Technically, only part of the house, the rear wing, belonged to Macy. In 1836 it was sold to John H. Shaw, a

Above, top: The house is raised templelike on a high basement foundation, and has a classically symmetrical façade. An Ionic portico creates a most dignified entranceway.
Above: The living room, filled with sophisticated fabrics in exuberant colors and patterns, is furnished with upholstered pieces you want to sink into. Period pieces and faux-finished accents help to create a feeling of timelessness. Rose Cumming chintz has been used to create deliciously extravagant window curtains—with lining fabric so exquisite you want to turn the edges back so it won't be missed.
Right: A garage was converted into a lovely garden room. Its faux-stone floor was painted by the owner, as was a marbleized coffee table.

whaling merchant, who was a partner in a firm that owned a candle factory. He moved it to the rear of the lot so it could become the ell, or wing, for the Federal-style house he was building. During that same year, men were paving the main business section of Main Street with cobblestones. One can imagine the bustle of activity back then, much as we know it on island today.

Most Nantucketers can't remember anyone owning the house before the Leeds Mitchell family occupied it from the early 1900s until 1986.

For four years in the early 1980s, Jon and I had the good fortune to live in this house while we were building an addition to our own house on Union Street. So it was with feelings of nostalgia that we visited the house after it was later restored. What we found convinced us that, before long, everyone will come to know this as the house that Dorothy and Dusty Slover restored to its present and rightful elegance.

When the Slovers bought 77 Main Street in 1986, not much had been done to it for fifty years. It was just waiting for a sensitive restoration. While structurally sound, the house needed updated electrical and plumbing systems, insulation, new fixtures, new bathrooms (there are seven in all), and the rebuilding of all eight fireplaces. Painting proved to be the most expensive and time-consuming part of the job. There are literally dozens of coats of glaze on the interior walls and ceilings. They also rebuilt a rotting kitchen (part of the original ell), restored the back bedrooms above it, and decorated the entire three floors. The work

Far left: The library is intimate and comfortably luxurious. Its walls have been finished to complement the leather wing chairs, which were among the furnishings that came with the house and were worth the effort of restoring. Tapestry pillows, rich in texture and color, capture the prevailing tone of the room.
Above: A sense of grandeur pervades the dining room, where sixteen can be accomodated. When the sun streams through the tall windows, the room positively glows.
Left: An unusual collection of carved jade marbles and shagreen eyeglass cases is on display in the Slover library. The cases once belonged to Chinese peasants.

Left: The graceful central stairway, with its sweeping curve up to the second floor, is one of the features that sold the Slovers on the house. The bold checkerboard floor contrasts with the pale pink curved walls. Few people would have the courage to make such a bold statement in a central passage, but this is just a hint of what's to come.

Right: The bright modern kitchen is the hub of activity when the Slover children are home. The scrubbed-pine farm table is just right for informal family meals. Glossy white cabinets team up with brass hardware to make the kitchen look as streamlined as a ship's galley.

took three years. Dorothy credits the uncompromising level of excellence found in the Nantucket craftsmen for the success of its restoration. "In fact," she says, "they were responsible for raising my level of consciousness regarding other areas of the job that were not part of their work."

A tour through this Main Street house would surely dazzle most tourists, for it is indeed a treat that goes beyond the mere architecture of the place. This is a house where the graceful style of living has returned and all things lovely and beautiful have come to rest. The house is what it is today because of the vision, talents, and unbounded energy of its current mistress.

Interior details such as the generous molding and black marble fireplace mantels in the main rooms are distinctly Federal. These rooms can only be described as imposing, with their high ceilings and extra-tall windows. Dorothy has decorated with respect to tradition and authenticity, but has placed this house at the height of current fashion.

Everything Dorothy Slover puts her hand to expresses a single-minded aesthetic discipline. As a graduate of the Isabel O'Neil Studio

Workshop Foundation, Dorothy is a master craftswoman in the art of the painted finish. The house is an outstanding example of how she has applied her skills to every detail with an unequalled combination of high-quality materials, superior workmanship, and the sheer beauty of good design.

The kitchen is the only room in the house that was completely rebuilt. "We wanted to give something back to the house," Dorothy explains. "We felt that the kitchen cabinets should be made as finely as everything else here and built to last forever." Working with a kitchen designer in Washington, D.C., where she lives part of the year, Dorothy then employed architect Mike Kepanash to oversee all design details for the installation.

When the Slovers undertook the restoration of the house, everyone they knew advised them to remove the wing originally built by Macy. Much to her credit, Dorothy instinctively knew that this could be the most charming part of the house. Reached from a back stairway, these rooms were probably used by

John H. Shaw's household help back in the 1800s. They had easy access to the kitchen below and could serve the family unobtrusively. "They were tiny, low-ceilinged rooms," Dorothy says, "but nothing had rotted here the way it had in the kitchen. These rooms simply needed to be restored."

But this is not the end of the tour, for there are more surprises. On the third floor, there was once an attic. From there you could climb a ladder to the roofwalk atop the house and scan the entire town. This attic space is where the Slovers created a suite of rooms. And, to Mike Kepanash's credit, all the rooms were planned around the roofwalk stairway in the middle of it all. This is a true aerie retreat, private and worth the climb.

A double garage was turned into a delightful garden room encircled with French doors, thus gaining access to the yard and garden beyond.

"The garden is always evolving," says landscape designer Lucinda Young. "This is a garden that you can relate to. It's nice to walk through or around it. It's never static," Lucinda says, adding that the brickwork de-

fines the plantings with the right amount of formality.

Dorothy says, "When you redo a house you should let it speak to you as you go along. In this way you will be well guided." The Slover family is quite proud of their home. It has been tastefully restored so that it is beautiful and comfortable in the twentieth century without losing respect for its nineteenth-century heritage.

Above, left: The bedroom over the library belongs to the Slovers' son. The blue walls to enhance the rich, dark wood furniture. The rosettes at each corner of the generous molding are architectural details typical of a Federal house. Paneled shutters at the windows eliminate the need for curtains.
Above, center: The old-fashioned back bathroom was brought up to twentieth-century standards, but the charm of the nineteenth century has not been lost. The original clawfoot bathtub is still here, though conveniently accompanied by a shower. A small window offers a view of Main Street, which hasn't changed much from when the house was first built.
Above, right: Everything in the third-floor retreat has been painted "pure" white. The use of a raspberry print adds a note of dazzling color. Who could resist the curl-up allure of the cushioned window seat, especially under a window set high among the treetops?
Right: In one of the Slovers' daughter's bedrooms, floral fabrics are used to give the room a feminine lushness. Dorothy finished the walls with an intricate, striped, blue-and-white glazing.

PLAIN
AND SIMPLE
STYLE

Mill Street is one of those lanes that people love to wander down and discover. It feels the way Nantucket probably did back in the eighteenth century. If it's evening and the lights are on and the shutters open, we might catch a discreet glimpse inside, for we are forever fascinated with the lure of the past. We would not be disappointed here.

Built around 1790, this two-and-a-half-story shingle house on Mill Street is typical of Nantucket houses around the time of the American Revolution. The facade, with its twelve-over-twelve and nine-over-nine-paned windows, a front door with transom, and a ridge chimney, is characteristic of these early houses. The interior is a testament to the Quaker creed, which held a belief in the fundamental necessities for basic comfort, but scorned all luxuries or frills. Good craftsmanship was expected, adornment unacceptable.

The typical Nantucket house was set right at the edge of the street. As families grew and space was needed, the only place to go with

Top left: An early Quaker-style house on Mill Street.
Left: Subtle shades of yellow create a warm environment in the sunlit master bedroom. Anne has created an inviting setting between the front windows: a wicker chair with a mohair throw woven at The Nantucket Looms, a fabric-covered table holding an assortment of framed family photographs, a bouquet of flowers from the garden, and a Nantucket basket filled with potpourri. An antique Shaker christening dress hangs from a peg on the wall.
Above: The main feature of the living room is the pine-paneled fireplace wall. Since most fireplaces on Nantucket were originally larger than those found in homes on the mainland, it is logical to assume that the paneled wall was a later addition.
Right: A restrained approach to decorating in the dining room grants architectural elements their full due. The quilt on the wall is called "Ocean Waves." Anne's garden provides for ever-changing arrangements on the table.

Left: The simple understated design of an Amish quilt is the focal point at this end of the living room. The hooked rug of undulating waves and soft, muted colors enhances the charm of the original pine floorboards, which have softened and aged to a rich and warm glow. A piece of pottery made by Anne's son is the perfect single element for display on the pine chest. Above: A small structure, used for storage and potting, is nestled at the edge of the garden. Roses creep up the shingles and sprawl over the trellised roof. Gardening is very much a part of the Nantucket landscape. Anne's garden, with its wide beds of perennial and annual flowers, is a source of enjoyment all season long.

additions, known in Nantucket as "warts," was back or out to the side. The side ell, added here by previous owners, expanded the house to include a laundry and sitting room downstairs with extra bedrooms on the second floor.

While the house meets the street, once inside it's easy to step back in time and imagine a family of Quakers going about the daily business of living.

Much to the credit of its present owners, Anne and James Grieves, the house retains its unyielding classic simplicity, keeping the world at bay. Only the kitchen has been modernized, but not in such a way as to be out of step with the rest of the house. It still maintains a country flavor, and Anne hopes to remodel it once again to meet the demands of her business, "Take Five," which offers cooking classes in her home.

Anne's attitude about her cooking is no different from the way she lives. There is nothing gimmicky or trendy about her approach to decorating or entertaining. The non-essentials are eliminated, very much in the Nantucket tradition. "For me, cooking is an art," Anne says. "It is also a gift of love that I share with my family and friends. I know more people would enjoy cooking if it were simpler. My recipes modify the ingredients down to five. With five ingredients you can prepare sophisticated, healthy, and delicious food."

Because of its pure and simple style, living here is easy and comfortable. The preserved wide floorboards, paneled shutters at the windows, paneled wall in the living room, and the dining-room fireplace with its oven intact, are some of the

outstanding features that make the house more charming today than it might have been considered when it was first built.

The Puritan starkness of the architecture is enhanced by a straightforward approach to decorating, which is softened and updated by the use of tasteful fabrics and well-chosen quilts on the walls. Anne consulted with expert Phyllis Haders when selecting the quilts, and a nautical theme seemed appropriate.

The house reflects the simple Quaker influence that professed restraint, decency, and spiritualism. Quakers believed that a house should serve a practical purpose and not be an object of beauty. There should be no adornment. While their houses were of a simple form and without much detail, they were well-proportioned. Employing a similar philosophy, Anne Grieves demonstrates in this house that a certain amount of restraint in the twentieth century can grant architectural elements their full due.

Left: The typical Nantucket oven next to the fireplace was used for cooking. The original nineteenth-century wood door can be seen inside. The area below was used for storage. Right: The wall in the upstairs hallway is dominated by a patchwork quilt with a compass design. As with most patchwork quilts, the blocks are formed of squares or triangles that make up each pattern. These early quilts are among the most prized collectibles because of their wonderful designs. Time adds significance to a quilt, as it has to this early Nantucket house.

ISLAND CRAFTS

The Nantucket lightship basket came into existence in the latter part of the nineteenth century. These tightly woven cane baskets were made by lightship keepers. There were many different sizes, depending on forms over which they were shaped. The most popular size today is the lady's pocketbook, which has become a Nantucket status symbol. Older baskets are among the most appreciated collectibles in island homes.

Native basketmakers Karl and Susan Chase Ottison say there are many fine crafters on the island and each has his or her own style. Many lightship purses are adorned with a carved or scrimshaw plaque.

Scrimshaw is the scribing of a design on a piece of ivory or bone. It is one of the first folk crafts originated by New England whalers who spent years at sea during colonial times. These sailors spent their leisure time drawing and scribing on whale's teeth and whalebone.

AN ARTIST'S HOME AND STUDIO

The entrance is practically right on the road at 13 West Dover Street, but if it weren't for the sign marked "Donn Russell Studio Loft" on the side of the fence, you'd probably miss it altogether. Stepping through the ivy-encrusted gate, one leaves the business of the town behind and enters a private world where time stands still. It's easy to linger here before entering the house or studio.

Like so many houses on Nantucket, this one needed a great deal of work when the artist bought it almost twenty years ago. Before it could be adequately reclaimed for comfortable living, Donn Russell and colleague Arthur Schaefer designed, remodeled, and shaped the house and gardens into a personal expression of their individual talents. Today the house is a reminder of how Nantucket used to be when it was a haven for artists whose first creative expressions were evidenced in their living spaces. The adjacent studio at the far end of the garden was added later.

Donn Russell is somewhat of a Renaissance man—a sculptor, artist, and printmaker, as well as an accom-

Above: Donn Russell has an extensive collection of vintage mechanical toys. Each one moves in its own unique way.
Center right: The entrance to Donn Russell's house and studio is at the edge of the street.
Bottom right: The entryway leads to a charming compact kitchen.
Far right: The curved wood-frame chairs, with their grey leather seats, were once used on a luxury liner. They are perfectly at home here, flanking an original Donn Russell cabinet that incorporates found weathered wood.

plished piano player, world traveler, and the director of a private foundation which supports experimental plays, dance, and film productions in New York City. His is a creative life, totally integrated, inspiring an approach toward refurbishing and furnishing the house.

Every nook and cranny of the space is a visual treat. Found objects discovered on beachcombing forays, weathered wood, and driftwood have been incorporated into the structure of the house. Mixed with Donn's sculptures, paintings, and pieces of furniture, the look is functional and aesthetic. Early Persian and Oriental rugs brought from his travels add to the balance and proportion of the furnishings.

Pleasing sounds in the house obliterate any intrusive noises beyond the morning-glory-covered windows facing the street. From the open kitchen door one hears the murmur of water trickling from the man-made pond and birds chirping in the surrounding trees.

Far left: The living room is an eclectic mix. Here the artist displays his own work with that of other Nantucket artists. The wooden screen to the left was made from weathered barrel tops. The base of the coffee table was once an old lobster trap. The lion's head sculpture on the driftwood table was part of a commissioned advertising campaign. Wide, worn floorboards, enhanced by many scatter rugs, add to the character of the room.
Above: The first floor of the studio is used as an office, guest room, and silk-screening studio. A narrow, winding stairway leads to the top floor where the artist creates the work that will ultimately be displayed and sold at his print gallery on Old South Wharf.
Left: The concentrically designed garden between the house and the studio is nurtured by Arthur Schaefer. Each summer The Nantucket Artist's Association sponsors a tour of artists' studios that ends with refreshments served here.

COMBINING THE OLD AND THE NEW

When Julie Sanford bought the house at 19 Lily Street, it was like so many older Nantucket houses that had been altered over the years—not very interesting and in need of updating. As an interior designer, Julie had no difficulty imagining how to remodel the Federal-style house for a family with two young children.

The house has a clapboard front, shingle sides, a high brick basement, end chimneys, a four-bayed façade, a doorway with sidelights, dormers, a new wing to one side, and a double "friendship" stairway.

Julie instinctively knew she could give this house a look that would retain its architectural distinctions while accommodating a contemporary lifestyle. Classically handsome furniture, country crafts, original art, local antiques, and the owner's unfussy approach combined to rekindle the nineteenth-century spirit of this historic house on a delightful in-town street. Julie has achieved a house that is comfortable, charming, and uncluttered, with rooms for the children to be themselves and other,

Above: This early house on Lily Street is one-and-three-quarter-stories tall with front dormers in each of the two bedrooms upstairs.
Above, right: An arrangement of flowers adds a finishing touch to this charming living-room alcove. There is a fireplace to the right and another in the dining room.
Right: The dining room is lighthearted. Julie's inspired wall treatment offers a random pattern of gold stars on a white background. It is just right with the collection of furniture and accessories: handpainted chairs around the table, a Victorian doll house in one corner, a display of whimsical folk art, "Hummock Pond Perch" on the wall, and a collection of colored glass lamps on the sea chest.

Left: The double dormer in the bedroom creates an alcove for a dressing table filled with favorite mementos. The ribbon wallpaper border runs around the entire room. The hooked rug, depicting several Nantucket houses, picks up the green and pink colors of the room.
Right: Most of the furniture in the house, such as the four-poster bed, belonged to Julie's family. An antique grained bureau holds one of her favorite glass lamps.

more formal areas for adult entertaining. These are rooms you can live with for a long time.

Julie has a sense of what makes an interior work. Her eclectic mix of old and new seems appropriate for a house that is one hundred and fifty years old.

This is not just a summer home, but one that is lived in year-round, and as such, it changes with the seasons. In the summer, living here is carefree and casual. Doors are left open to the yard and garden, letting the outdoors in. Children are always coming and going.

It's bright and cheerful, due in part to the use of colorful fabrics and wallpaper. The spatter-painted wood floors are the perfect backdrop for Julie's assortment of hooked rugs. There is plenty of visual stimulation here, and in the winter when everything turns inward, the house becomes warm and cozy because the rooms are well-proportioned and each relates well to the rest of the house.

Julie's office is off the center hall. It's a delightfully feminine room with evidence of her work everywhere. Swatches of fabric are piled on a bench, pretty fabric-covered boxes are used to organize notes on the various houses she's currently decorating, and an antique desk holds

Above: The front hall is papered with a yellow floral print.

Left: In an older house, the bathroom is typically at the top of the stairs. This room is filled with country treasures: a framed quilt hangs on one wall, early cloth dolls line the window ledge, and an old-fashioned clawfoot tub holds a lightship basket filled with the necessities for a leisurely steep.

Above, left: Dating from the early nineteenth century, the cut-font lamps once burned kerosene. While they have been converted for electricity, they are no less valuable. Lamps such as these are prized for their beautiful design and craftsmanship.

Right: A white iron bed is tucked under the eaves in a daughter's bedroom. The antique patchwork quilt is sewn in a star pattern, a favorite pattern of early quiltmakers. The farm-scene hooked rug and cloth dolls add to the country images that evoke earlier days.

an appointment book with every hour of her busy day accounted for. Julie's organized approach to business makes it easy for her clients to express their individuality. Particularly creative when it comes to color and texture, she has guided many Nantucket home owners in their search for wallpaper, fabrics, and accessories that look right together.

Years ago people gave little thought to decorating their summer homes on Nantucket. Today, however, more people are aware of good design and while they want their homes to be comfortable and carefree, they also want them to be aesthetically pleasing. Entertaining is a way of life here and creating a pretty environment in which to do so is part of Nantucket style. Since so many people own summer homes and are away more than they are here, they want to get the most out of the summer months. Having a design consultant like Julie Sanford, who is sensitive about island living, assures that they will spend less time choosing fabrics and more time enjoying their environment.

FLOWERS

Nantucketers are passionate about their gardens. June is the month when everything begins to bloom all over the island. Fences can barely contain the daisies, cosmos, coreopsis, black-eyed Susans, day lilies, and hollyhocks. 'Sconset cottages are laden with roses that climb up shingles and sprawl over trellised rooftops.

Wildflowers grow all over the island. Queen Anne's lace, chicory, and lavender turn the island into a blanket of delicate color. From June until late fall the island puts on quite a flower show.

ON THE BLUFF

Below, top: A family home sits high on the bluff at Siasconset.
Below, bottom: Italian black swan figures sit in a window niche off the hallway.
Right: Island decorator Gary Knight worked with the owners to design an all-white interior to take advantage of the spectacular views.

Sitting high in 'Sconset and looking out in all directions, one is instantly reminded that this is an island thirty miles out to sea. Sunlight dances off the whitecaps and brightens the green foliage shielding the property from the bluff that drops to the water's edge. The silence is broken by the rhythmic sounds of waves and the squawk of a seagull. This is where Bonnie and Elliott Barnett live.

What you see from every room can only be described as "a knockout view." And while the house itself is tailor-made for summer living, the real star of this house is the sparkling blue Atlantic Ocean, which practically wraps itself around the property. The living room appears to extend right outdoors to where the lush green lawns meet the edge of the bluff.

This spectacular home proves there's nothing neutral about white. Simple, pure, and sophisticated, white expresses contemporary elegance throughout this home. The interior is open and freeflowing, designed for full communion with the glorious views.

Working with island decorator Gary Knight, the owners chose everything in the house with impeccable sensitivity toward this end. The subtle white-on-white sofas and chairs, painted furniture, and displayed objects are never overwhelming. The success of using all white comes from the variety of shapes and textures in this natural setting. By keeping the background relatively simple, the art pieces and artifacts are shown to their best advantage. Most of all, the give and take between the owners and the decorator resulted in a very creative collaboration.

Bonnie is a busy lady. In the off-season, when she's not presiding over the activities of her family in Nantucket, she's attending to matters in her capacity as a knowledge-able and respected art dealer in Florida. Naturally, when she and Elliott redesigned the house (a house this elegant doesn't just happen!), art played an important part in the interior design. The latest books about art and artists are neatly stacked on shelves and tables throughout the house.

As you come in through the front

Above and right: The two decks at ground level and the one off the master bedroom command unobstructed views of the ocean. The white wicker furniture and masses of potted pink geraniums contribute to an atmosphere of serenity evocative of an earlier, more romantic era.
Top far right: The sunroom is an addition just off the living room. It leads directly to a deck where the family comes to relax. They've combined light wicker furniture with sculpture, art, and island crafts. Nesting baskets and the one filled with dried flowers on the table were made by native basketmakers Karl and Susan Chase Ottison. The Barnetts also own an impressive collection of antique lightship baskets by Nantucket's original basketmaker, José Reyes.
Bottom far right: The coffee table in the living room holds a selective arrangement of natural-colored artifacts, including a basket of ostrich eggs, and primitive pieces.

door, the space opens up immediately to the second floor, lifting your eyes to high ceilings and a gracious stairway. As you walk through it, the house unfolds like a well-conceived gallery. It is an unusual style for Nantucket and one that makes this home unique. The black-and-white art gracing the walls of the house adds to its drama.

The house is clearly designed for entertaining, as well as for enjoying art. Groups of people can sit in this living room and feel relaxed. And while it's gracious and elegant, it's also comfortable and homey. Bonnie and Elliott have an intuitive sense of family and have created a home that accommodates everyone's summer activities perfectly.

When Bonnie and Elliott bought the house, there were two little bedrooms upstairs. It seemed only logical to remove a wall in order to create one large room. In this way, the bed could be placed at one end to create a comfortable and spacious sleeping area that includes a mirrored dressing room and bath.

Left: Favorite mementos, framed family photographs, and white ceramic lightship baskets designed by island artist George Davis line the bench under the bedroom windows. The ocean view is enjoyed from the overstuffed chairs in the sitting area.
Right: The spacious foyer is open to the second floor. Black-and-white art lines the walls, giving the room a special, gallery-like feeling.

The rest of the room became an open sitting area. A sofa and two oversized chairs are arranged to take advantage of the view, where sailboats occasionally dot the horizon. Whether the Barnetts are relaxing, reading, or lying in bed, the ocean is ever-present.

There is more to this house, of course—a few bedrooms, a children's wing added last year over the two-car garage, an unbelievable kitchen, and fabulous bathrooms—but had we stayed here much longer, we might never have left.

AN EARLY HOME ON MILK STREET

Dating from about 1750, this house has had several owners over the last two hundred and fifty years. Changes and additions over time have altered it somewhat, culminating in what is today a very livable and comfortable home for a well-known painter/sculptor.

In 1784, Tristram Starbuck sold the house to John Coleman. Upon his death, it passed to the Macy family. Deeds described the property as "being to the northwards of the Wind Mills," and included other buildings that came with the house, one of which was a cooper's shop. Benjamin Coffin Chase wanted to buy the house in 1840, but first insisted that the cooper's shop be removed. It seems only fitting that years later a separate building, the present owner's studio, should be part of the existing property.

A typical Nantucket house, this one follows a pattern of other houses built right after the earlier lean-tos. It is known as a three-quarter house because the door is off-center. The original two front rooms and parlor were moved from

the town of Sherburne, and the house was turned so that the original front door is now in back of the house. At the time this house was built, Nantucketers were beginning to move away from building their houses facing toward the sun, in favor of facing them toward the street.

The house was originally built with the wood from shipwrecks. Most of this wood still remains. In the living room the old beams and doors combine happily with new paneling and bookcases where a large cooking fireplace once existed.

The interior doors, with glass transoms above them, are one of the house's more prominent features. They were considered a necessity for spotting fires, should one break out in the next room.

Once a small bedroom, now the gracious entryway sets the tone of the house. It is at once contemporary in style and traditional in comfort. The heavy door closes behind you and the solidness of the house makes you forget that it stands on a busy in-town street. Everything

Above: Mature flowering bushes, trees, and shrubbery abound on the property of this eighteenth-century, in-town house. A rosy brick path curves from the house to the studio where the owner-artist creates the work that is shown in galleries in New York City and Nantucket. Masses of flowers spill out over the edges of their beds and onto the path, creating just the right mood for making the transition from home to work.
Right: Soft colors and textures create an appropriate background for the art and objects displayed in the living room at the rear of the house. One of the artist's paintings hangs over the sofa and a piece of her sculpture is displayed on the coffee table. The needlepoint pillow on the sofa is the artist's rendition of her house, and won first prize at The Nantucket Artist's Association craft exhibit.

Top: The sharply winding back stairway is typical of these early houses. The underside of the garret stair has been plastered in a smooth curve. This is an interesting area for displaying modern art by local artists Sterling Mulbry and Linda Zola.
Above: The walls in the foyer are painted the palest shrimp color, making everything rather soft, warm, and rosy. The original beams, moldings, and trim are enhanced with glossy white paint.
Far right: On the dining-room sideboard, a sculpture by the owner shares space with pottery by Piero Fenci and two beautiful carvings of reindeer made from pieces of ivory.

draws your attention, making you aware that this house is different from most homes of its vintage.

This is a home that's easy to live in, and reflects the well-traveled owner's confident style. Her fine collection of antiques and art, as well as an impressive group of sculptures, mix well with the elegant furnishings, contemporary fabrics and colors, and native crafts. As a result, the house exhibits a decorator's eye for detail, a collector's taste, and an artist's concern with color.

It is unusual to see modern works in such an early house. The owner appreciates art and her home reflects and respects the creative process. It is a tribute to this artist that, while she displays her own paintings and sculpture throughout every room, it is not only hers that one finds here. In fact, most of the work is by artists and sculptors whose work she simply enjoys living with. She might hang a painting by local artist Bobby Bushong alongside a Picasso or a Miro. The owner has spent a lifetime helping to promote the arts and supporting talented artists by buying their

work. Indeed, the careers of many young island artists were given a boost as a result of this woman's interest.

There's a wonderful play among the objects in these rooms. Who but an artist would keep fresh flowers on a table under the painting of the bouquet? Perhaps it's because this is one of the artist's own paintings, and Nantucket's natural environment is so much a part of her work.

When she isn't in her studio, the artist spends most of her time in the new living room. It is here that she relaxes or entertains friends. There's a formal living room in the front of the house, but this is a brighter and friendlier room where the sunlight streams in most of the day. Tabletops are forested with groupings of sculpture, books, vases, figurines, familiar old possessions, and objects that include not just exquisite rareties, but also humble souvenirs and beloved reminders of friends, family, and colleagues. The result is unstudied charm—the kind of collecting pleasure that transcends mere attainment.

Left: A large cooking fireplace once filled the wall of one end of the living room. New paneling and built-in bookcases were added by the present owner.

Above: A table by the window holds freshly cut lilies from the garden, two small lightship baskets made on Nantucket, and a goat figure, found during one of the owner's many summers spent in Positano. Knotted boat line is a clever way to hold back the delicate curtains.

Right: The coral centerpiece holds an arrangement of garden flowers. They go perfectly with the floral pattern of the china.

Left: Original house details, such as the slanted floor and ceiling, can be seen in the front living room. The sculpture on the mantel is by Italian artist Canestrari. The small brass piece is by Dmitri Hudzi, whose work is shown in New York and Boston galleries.

Above: The bottom of the winding back stairway is a great place for the display of folk art, such as the wooden St. Francis by artist Ben Ortega of Santa Fe, and a few lightship purses. The darkened color of the baskets attests to their age and makes them quite valuable.

Right: The upstairs sitting room is used as an office. An arrangement of sofa and chairs around the fireplace makes it a cozy room off the master bedroom. A needlepoint pillow is one of the artist's creations, as is the painting of Positano. Decoys, primitive toys from Mexico, and Balinese fish decorate the mantel.

AN AMERICAN CLASSIC

Owning a humble, tumble-down house on an island is one thing, turning it into one's castle is quite another. If the people of Nantucket share a weakness, it is for just these kinds of odds.

When it comes to finding and restoring a gem of an early Nantucket house, it takes an astute couple like Jinny and Joe Beaulieu, who are no novices when it comes to this sort of thing. They once owned and restored a 1700s house in western Massachusetts, and their current off-island home was built in 1860.

Located at 29 Union Street, one of Nantucket's grand historic in-town streets, this two-and-a-half-story house was built in 1806 by a ship's carpenter named Clovis Black. When the Beaulieus first looked at it in 1974, it had been unoccupied for years and was a wreck. Since it is located just a few doors down from our house, we passed it often on our way to town. Our nickname for number 29 was "the haunted house."

You couldn't go inside the house for fear of falling through the rotted floorboards of the upstairs rooms to the ground floor. The kitchen, once a wart on the back of the house, had rotted away and fallen off. A wing on one side of the house, with a room downstairs and a bedroom above, was a mere shell. We speculated that if anyone were crazy enough to buy the place, they'd surely remove that section altogether. The bathrooms were nonexistent, all the windows were broken, the sills had rotted away, and the whole place looked like a bombed-out building in a war-devastated city. This was the sort of house that real-estate agents would call a real "fixer upper."

But, lucky for this house, the Beaulieus possess first-hand knowledge of restoration and understood what was needed to turn it into a first-rate home. Considering the shape it was in, it's surprising that the work was completed in only two years. There isn't an artist on the island today who doesn't choose this house as a subject for his or her canvas.

Thirty-two windows and thirteen

Top: A classic eighteenth-century house on historic Union Street, just a few steps from Main Street. A low herb garden is contained by the winding brick path that leads from the front gate to the side kitchen door.
Above: The antique cabinet in the kitchen holds many interesting objects. The lightship baskets are used often and the lambs are part of a collection lining a fireplace mantel in one of the six upstairs bedrooms.
Right: In this country-style kitchen, old baskets hang from the rafters within easy reach.

Left: Antique containers are part of Jinny's kitchen collection.
Right: An early butter churn stands in the door-way, which leads to a delightful patio encircled by a garden that is vibrant with color all summer long. Hollyhocks grow close to the house and foxglove, peonies; pansies, poppies, and petunias spill over deep flower beds onto the brickwork. A vegetable garden is tended right alongside the flowers.

doors were replaced. The plumbing and electrical systems were installed and the entire house was re-shingled. The only good news came when the top floorboards were removed and they found wide pine floorboards in restorable shape beneath. Six fireplaces had been completely covered with cement and brick and, once uncovered, new hearths were laid and all six fireplaces restored to working order.

It must have taken strong instincts and a great deal of courage to restructure an entire wing of the house, but today it is a country kitchen that is functional and hospitable. Like the rest of the house, this room reflects Jinny's ongoing passion for collecting antiques. Her boxes, containers, tins, early housewares objects, and baskets hanging from rafters reveal a keen understanding of the value of things which have stood the test of time.

A SETTING FOR A MARITIME COLLECTION

This is an unusual style of Nantucket house, not typical of the architecture found here. It was designed and built by Kenneth Taylor, who lived on the island in the 1920s and 1930s and was greatly concerned with the welfare of the island. Upon his death in the early 1940s, he left five thousand dollars to the town for the establishment of the Nantucket Foundation. The money was to be used as the town saw fit, to serve the community in the best possible way.

In 1945, the Macy Warehouse on Straight Wharf, long finished with the business of storing whale oil for which it was intended in the 1800s, was put up for sale. It was decided that the best use of the Foundation money was for the purchase of this historic building and the little one next door, in order to establish a multifaceted art gallery and workshop. The building was renamed The Kenneth Taylor Gallery.

In the beginning, the gallery exhibited art brought in from New York City's Metropolitan and Whitney museums. In its first year of operation,

there were candlelight talks by writers Thornton Wilder and Tennessee Williams, among other illustrious names.

By 1952 the gallery evolved into The Nantucket Artists Association, providing exposure for local as well as off-island artists. The gallery was deeded to The Nantucket Historical Association in 1984, and by October 1988 the Nantucket Artists Association moved into its newly renovated headquarters in The Little Gallery, the building next door. Kenneth Taylor's name was removed from the old Macy Warehouse to make way for the changing times.

Though structurally in good shape when the present owners bought the house, it needed a bit of revamping. After living in the house for several years, the owners made minor changes to the exterior when the living room was enlarged slightly. Not wanting to change the scale or design of the house, the owners simply pushed it out a bit by installing two bay windows in one wall and French doors at the end. This expanded the space and

Top: This unusual in-town house was built in the 1920s by Kenneth Taylor.
Above: Maritime antiques are displayed in the dining room. Oval nesting baskets were made by native lightship keepers in the eighteenth century. Nantucket rolling pins were made of beechwood and ivory or completely of bone. This one has an ivory star at one end and a half moon at the other end. A beautifully carved hand holds the bowl of an ivory pipe.
Right: The living room is a return to classic interior decoration with a mix of finely upholstered sofas and antique tables and chairs. Honey-colored walls give the room a subtle glow. It's a wonderful, timeless room designed to accommodate large gatherings or intimate groups. Old and new nesting baskets live in harmony. In time, the new baskets, made by the Ottisons, will be as dark as the old and just as valuable. A ship's model, small baskets, and a lady's purse with an ivory scrimshaw plaque rest on the end table. The magnifying glass sports a carved ivory handle.

Left: Of special interest in the dining room is the curved ceiling. In keeping with this, the present owners restructured the straight lintel of the doorway with a curved top. The arched paneling over the fireplace continues the design detail. An early Nantucket lightship basket holding flowers is just part of the owners' extensive sea-related collection.

Right: Carved canes and walking sticks fill an umbrella stand by the front door. The scrimshaw ivory plaque on top of the owner's purse is an illustration of the house done by respected artisan and native scrimshander Nancy Chase.

Overleaf: These one-of-a-kind canes and walking sticks (some of which belonged to Nantucket sea captains) have elaborately carved ivory-and-bone handles and were considered decorative accessories in the eighteenth and nineteenth centuries.

brought light into the room without altering the existing structure's classic lines.

The house's open porch was enlarged by adding an additional curved archway for an attractive outdoor sitting area and graceful entrance. Well-conceived landscaping also plays a part in the exterior appeal. A winding stone path, flanked by shrubbery and flower beds, leads from the gate at the edge of the property to the front porch.

When you enter this house it feels solid and well-built, as though it will last forever, the way a family home ought to. And this is what the present owners appreciate about it. The layout is traditional, with a center hall and stairway straight ahead. To the left, the living room runs the full length of the house from front to back. In back of the stairs there's a den for reading or watching television. The dining room sits to the right of the center hallway, and in back of that a bedroom and bath. The kitchen, off the dining room, leads to the side and back yards.

The entryway is the hub from which all activity stems. But it is

also a room unto itself, mainly because it houses most of the marine antiques. When you arrive here, you don't want to go any further until you've absorbed it all. And there is plenty to take in. A floor-to-ceiling cabinet is built into one wall. The unit is lit from inside and the pieces are carefully arranged on each of the glass shelves. In this way it lets you appreciate the entire collection as a whole, yet each object stands on its own. Discernment, knowledge, and taste are the cornerstones on which this impressive collection was built. Every carved ivory or bone piece has a history and is beautifully made.

The top shelf holds "prisoner of war" models made of bone. These were carved by French prisoners of war in England at the time of the Napoleonic Wars, during their incarceration aboard ships on the Thames or in prisons. These were poor but intelligent souls, and with skill and ingenuity they used the bones from their meals to make and rig ship models. Fine carving was a tradition in France and the high standard of the prisoners' work distinguishes their ship models from sailors' handiwork. Often mistaken for scrimshaw, it's sometimes impossible to differentiate the work.

Jagging wheels or pie crimpers, used for decorating pastry, date to the eighteenth century. The oldest known Nantucket ivory jagging wheel is dated 1773. Made of ivory, whale bone, or baleen and mahogany, they showed a variety of subject matter, as seen here. The fancier jagging wheels, some with mother-of-pearl inlay, were valued more as works of art than as tools.

Far left: A built-in cabinet in the entryway holds an impressive collection of antique maritime carvings.

Above: Staffordshire pieces line a window shelf in the dining room. A swift made of whale ivory or bone, with floral scrimshaw designs, took the skills of a master craftsman. The bone sewing basket and knitting needles with carved lady's boots on the ends are prized collectibles. A little knob turns the carved spinning jenny.

Left: Jagging wheels, or pie crimpers, used for decorating pastry, date to the eighteenth century. The oldest known Nantucket ivory jagging wheel is dated 1773. Made of ivory, whale bone, or baleen and mahogany, they showed a variety of subject matter, as seen here. The fancier jagging wheels, some with mother-of-pearl inlay, were valued more as works of art than as utilitarian objects.

DOORS

Doors reveal a great deal about the style of a house and the period in which it was built. The earliest lean-tos, of which there are eighty on the island, have simple board-and-batten doors. A transom window over the doorway is the place where one might find blown-glass witch's balls on display.

During the Federal and Greek-Revival periods, the doorways became more elaborate, with porticoes, side windows, and often a fan window above the door. These doorways are imposing and much grander than those found on simple Quaker houses.

THE CAPTAIN RICHARD GARDNER HOUSE, 1724

"We're just caretakers of the houses we live in," Jessica Woodle says of her early Nantucket house, "and responsible for appreciating what is here and respecting what was." A visit to this early lean-to house renews one's understanding of the importance of preservation and a respect for things which have stood the test of time. It is a journey into the culture of our New England beginnings.

The house was built in 1724 for Captain Richard Gardner. The back of the house faces West Chester Street, one of Nantucket's oldest streets, and the Lily Pond area. Captain Gardner was lost at sea, and for the next hundred years there is no record of who lived here. Whaling Captain Priam Pease Brock bought the house in 1822, only to live in it for one year before going down with his crew on the Nantucket whaler *Franklin.* However, his son lived to see his own daughter and her daughter born in the house. After his death in 1908, his daughter, Annie Brock Bowen, lived here for sixteen years, making it one hundred

Top left: The front of the house overlooks the Lily Pond area. Early Nantucket houses were always built to face the sun.
Above: Roses climb up the trellis by the front door, and rare swirling glass witches' balls, once used to ward off evil spirits, line the shelf of the transom over the door.
Left: The kitchen doors lead to a delightful private patio surrounded by a natural wall of high hedges.
Right: The fireplace, discovered behind a smaller one, is the largest in the house and dominates one wall of the dining room. The old oak beams show to full advantage here, with a single great beam over the fireplace providing the dominant feature of this gracious room. Pewter plates lining the mantel are part of an extensive collection found throughout the house.

Left: The weathered blue highchair came with the house when Jessica bought it. Perhaps it belonged to one of Captain Brock's grandchildren. It is a beautifully proportioned, well-designed piece of furniture, as much a treasure as the finer pieces in the house.
Right: The desk and many of the things on it belonged to Jessica when she was a child. She has used it all her life. There is a treenware cup, some pewter pieces, a magnifying glass with an ivory handle, and a bone cup etched with a picture of a whale and ship and inscribed: *Presented to holder, Slocum Captn from members of his crew on completion of his voyage: Apr. 27, 1875—Aug. 27 1877.* The world map over the desk is painted and embroidered on fine-weave linen. Framed pictures are matted with bargello needlework. The valances over the windows are early examples of fine crewel embroidery.

and one years that the same family occupied the house. While changes were made with each new generation, these were superficial, and for all those years the original house endured.

Jessica enjoys showing people through the house. As a member of the Nantucket Garden Club, she has opened her home for many years to share it with visitors to the island.

The house can be approached one of two ways—up a wide stone driveway to the side yard, or through an arched privet to a narrow stone path, then across an expanse of lawn to the kitchen or front door, depending on which way you turn. Its front door opens onto sweeping lawns and a well-manicured garden beyond. It is incredible to imagine that such lush surroundings exist at the edge of town. If you hadn't been looking for the house, you'd never know it was here. The house is set well back from the road behind a gracefully curved privet hedge, high enough to shield it from the mainstream eye, but low enough, where the curves

dip, to see through to the world beyond the lawn.

Friends often come to the kitchen door, which faces the road. It seems more friendly, not quite as imposing as walking around to the front. The patio on the driveway side of the house, off a later kitchen addition, is a delightful area enclosed by ivy-covered walls. Pots of white impatiens, petunias, and hanging pink geraniums surround the area, and seem so appropriate for the house. A cluster of potted herbs are within a step of the side kitchen door which leads to the brick patio.

Jessica's home is a friendly, open one, and there is always someone popping in for a visit. The house, while quite old, doesn't seem fossilized, but rather young and quite alive in spirit. One can imagine generations of little children growing up here and racing across the wide green lawns in a game of tag. In the middle of summer, with all the windows open wide, calm breezes blow through the house. It's pleasant here. The rooms are so comfortable you feel as though you've been here before.

What makes the house so livable is the collection of furnishings that have always been in Jessica's family. Every piece has a story to tell, and each object is more exquisite than the next. Everything here counts—and has survived for a reason. Surrounded by such impressive furnishings right from the start, it's no wonder that Jessica has such an appreciation for all that is here. Everything is displayed with a nonchalance that can leave a visitor breathless.

Throughout the house one finds examples of fine craftsmanship. The

Far left: The stairway's worn treads announce that these stairs have been used for a very long time.
Above: The heart-and-crown chair once belonged to a sea captain and now reposes next to a table that holds an ivory swift, or yarn winder, thought to be the most difficult of scrimshaw items to make. This freestanding model is rare. A banjo clock hangs on a door, no longer used, which once led to the borning room, now the library.
Left: The highback chairs with their ornate tapestry upholstery are seventeenth-century Italian. One can appreciate not only their fine workmanship, but also the fact that they exist in the twentieth century.

IN THE VILLAGE OF 'SCONSET

No one knows for sure exactly when this house was named, but its present owners think "None Too Big" suits it just fine. Ginny and Jay Hill were actually looking for waterfront property when they first came to Nantucket. But when they saw the dilapidated, unpretentious house that was once a general store smack in the old section of Siasconset, they were instantly intrigued. Today, after massive renovation, it reflects the combined creative efforts of an enormously energetic and aesthetically astute couple. The house is a little gem, nestled between other early structures that make up the heart of this village, where most of the houses have been occupied by the same family for generations.

The house sits sideways between Broadway and Center Street and one enters the front yard through a gate under an arched trellis. Something magical takes hold from the very moment you step into the yard. You are at once transported into a miniature wonderland, an oasis from the surrounding village. You

Top left: Something magical happens when you step through the garden gate.
Left: A room designed for three sons was created with a ship in mind. Everything is built-in, compact, and well-crafted. The beds are covered with canvas and everything on the walls relates to boating. Oversized cushions were made from early baby quilts.
Above: The table is set with tapestry placemats—a wonderful background for the blue Portuguese plates and rare Chinese bowls. The baleen-handled cutlery is fitting for a Nantucket home.
Right: This house had no fireplaces. Now it has two beehivelike hearths designed by the owners. This one, in the living room, has a raised hearth to accommodate a storage area for logs underneath.

stand transfixed, not wanting to go one step further before absorbing it all. It's hard to believe that none of this existed when the Hills first laid eyes on the property.

The old-fashioned charm of the low flower beds is reminiscent of that in an English cottage garden, filled with surprises. Perennials and herbs nestle right up against the house and are visually contained by a gently curving border created with clusters of stones gathered from Coatue, the arm of the island that juts out into the harbor. Different shades of green are unusual in this sandy soil. As avid gardeners, the Hills have carefully designed every area of the yard in such a delightfully uncontrived manner that it appears always to have been this way.

No creative opportunity has been overlooked. For example, the Hills wanted the deliberately irregular stone steps leading to the front door to look as though an old 'Sconset lady laid them long ago. Before the cement could dry, seashells were imbedded between the stones in just the right places. Large containers on either side of the steps overflow with verbena or daisies, depending on the mood desired, and are moved about at whim. At the kitchen door it seems natural to find a clay pot filled with herbs, for this is a family that likes to cook together. Everything here is totally integrated.

First it was the whaling people who lived in these little 'Sconset houses. Then it was the shepherds and farmers. The Hill house, which was never a whaling house, was supposed to have been brought here from Sankaty Light. Many additions have altered the structure since it was first built in the 1700s, and nothing original remains except a little buttery underneath the house.

Working with island architect J. Gwynne Thorsen, Ginny and Jay had this objective: to maintain the authenticity of the house as much as possible. Because all three of them had built boats, they came to the project with the same understanding. The interior of the house would be designed with an attitude stress-

Far left: The pine galley table in the kitchen was once part of an old Norwegian clipper ship. An island basket holds the wine. Herbs dug from the garden at summer's end add a simple elegance to the table setting and a wonderful scent to the room. The irregular tile floor adds to the country charm. A spiral stairway leads to the living room on the second floor.
Above, left: Bamboo fishing rods, wading boots, parasols, and a straw hat are within easy reach by the kitchen door.
Above, center: In earlier days, theatrical people came to perform at the 'Sconset Casino. A wonderful stenciled megaphone left over from those days is part of a grouping at one end of the living room. The pine side table holds clay pots planted with boxwood and surrounded by seashells. Ginny applied a wash of blue Portuguese paint to give the pots an Old World look. The Welsh fireplace chair, an early basket, and a primitive bird figure complement the simplicity of the room.
Above: Built-in sofas add to the boathouse quality found everywhere. The large, sumptuous cushions are covered in canvas and create the perfect setting for lounging or entertaining. A driftwood boat, formerly the top of a weathervane, adds just the right touch between the boat lights on the wall.

Left: A second spiral stairway leads from the front hallway to the upstairs bedrooms. A storage area under the stairs holds fishing gear in a milk-painted barrel. An oar from the Hill's boat and a variety of hats decorate one wall. An early basket is filled with hydrangeas.
Right: Lunch is a pleasant experience in the garden surrounded by trees and hedges just high enough to afford privacy without cutting off everyday sounds of activity. In the summer, the cushions are covered with a blue-and-white print and the table holds an ever-changing bouquet of island flowers. In the fall, the cushions are covered in earthy tones, with fresh pumpkins and squash adorning the tabletop.

ing the efficient use of space. It would be neat and organized and shipshape, with lots of built-ins, like the bunk beds which Jay and Ginny remember from his family's boathouse. They have followed their excellent instincts with impressive results. Mixed with the mysterious influence of European taste, every corner of the house is visually enticing and interacts easily with the activities of this busy family.

Back in the 1800s, a two-story addition was built across the gable end facing Broadway. That side of the house now comprises the downstairs kitchen and the second-floor living room, which is reached by a winding, wooden stairway. The kitchen, once the store, had a front porch which was removed. This room is now the hub of the house.

The kitchen is the perfect spot for an armful of wildflowers gathered from the fields and roadsides during a bike ride. Once home, Ginny reaches for an old basket hanging from a beam in the kitchen and fills it with the flowers she has spread across the table. Standing back, she

observes and confidently adds a few more, pulls a bunch over the edge to make the arrangement more casual, and—voilà!—it's ready for the table. That finished, she turns her attention to the next activity. Cooking a meal is done with the same love and attention, adding to the overall casual lifestyle which makes visitors and family so at home here.

The combination of white walls, pickled floors, scrubbed pine furniture (mostly Danish), uncluttered windows that are almost always open, and the use of white canvas with touches of blue, gives the house a clean, fresh feeling. No shades or draperies interfere with the relationship of the interior to the outside environment. Surprisingly, the lace curtains lend enough privacy while allowing light to filter through, creating wonderful patterns on the walls.

Far left: The master bedroom, which is reached from the living room through a rounded doorway, is all white with subtle touches of nautical blue. Books are conveniently at hand in the clever space provided inside the bedframe.
Above, left: The sea-blue towels in the bathroom are embroidered with the name of the house. Old Portuguese tiles frame the mirror over the sink.
Above: The potting shed was redesigned in just the right proportion for the yard. Window boxes brim with country flowers from spring through fall, and the small-paned, antique windows were brought here from the Cotswolds. Fleece vine grows up the trellised side and over the roof in uninhibited profusion.

ATTENTION
TO DETAIL

Built in 1802 by a Nantucket sea captain, this typical two-and-a-half-story house at 17 Union Street is now owned by Seymour and Miriam Mandell. The detail of the furnishings and a rich appreciation for history distinguish this in-town home.

The exterior of the house is striking, with its Shaker-blue clapboard façade, barn-red Federal door and shutters, and ivory trim. A slight variation from the typical Nantucket architecture is provided by the protruding molding over the doorway, taken from English architecture. Ivy covers its high pink foundation and a hedge affords just the right amount of privacy from the street. A gate leads into a "postage-stamp" garden by way of a rosy-pink brick walk. From early spring until late fall the pristine circular garden is vibrant with flowers and herbs. In the mid-eighteenth century, small English side gardens were creeping into existence despite the Quaker disdain for growing anything other than vegetables. We see small gardens like this everywhere in town.

The house is set close to the

Above: A typical sea captain's house c.1800.
Top right: A bird's nest was retrieved from the back yard once its occupants, a family of bluejays, had vacated the premises. The Mandells' respect for this basic architecture is evident in the display now holding three perfect wooden eggs. The natural color and texture of the nest are just right on the softened and aged surface of the table.
Right: A table is set with antique linens and freshly picked island flowers. This private garden-oasis is just a few steps from Main Street.
Far right: In the dining room, braided-silk tassels define the edges of the plaid taffeta valances and curtains. They are generously gathered at the top and puddle onto the wide planked floor. Island craftsperson Willa Embry, owner of Island Restoration, created the vinegar-grain finish on a sideboard.

Above: The living room has an Old World elegance. The luxurious tone comes from rich marbles and woods, as well as the soft pastel paint colors and refined fabrics. The wall chandeliers came from Sonny's family home in Philadelphia, as did much of the antique furniture. A purple needlepoint pillow on the wing chair and the palest pink mohair throw, handwoven at the Nantucket Looms, provide a counterpoint to the period tables.

Right: The tea table is filled with a vase of island flowers, a Staffordshire dog figure from the couple's collection, and china pieces that carry out the pink and floral theme.

Far right: In the front foyer, a black-and-white checkerboard floor is crisp and contemporary against traditional green molding, paneled door, window shutters, and trim. A pine blanket chest holds an early wood carved whirligig and the tall, twelve-over-twelve-paned windows brighten this welcoming area. Straw hats hung on the wall add a summertime feeling.

Overleaf: In the warm yellow sitting room there's a needlepoint pillow on the wing chair, a lightship basket topped with an unusual malachite plaque holding an ivory shell on the table, and a butter-soft, yellow mohair throw across the ottoman.

street, in keeping with the harmony of the times. That so many houses built during the 1800s were placed at the edge of the sidewalk is attributed to the pride Nantucketers felt for their town. They had no intention of being more isolated than they already were and from the start they were united on the attitude that Nantucket was a city. While it is small, they thought of it as urban. The streets they planned were not intended as country roads; Union Street in particular is one of the main thoroughfares, at least by Nantucket standards. The houses were built right to the sidewalk to unify the community. On a more practical note, when the houses were placed close together they served as windbreakers. The weathered grey shingles added further to the harmonious environment so popular with the Quakers. Later in the century, home owners began to add white trim and clapboard. The practice of defining the property with a fence completes the visual unity of the town.

The layout of this house is typical, but the interior design is anything but. The first thing you notice when you come through the front door is how everything is comfortably luxurious, willfully cluttered, artfully arranged, and not the least bit understated. This is an old house, but it isn't quaint or precious or stately. Everything is fresh, elegant, and pleasing to the eye. These rooms are romantic and civilized. Each one invites you graciously in.

Family antiques and modern treasures blend easily. Formal as well as relaxed furniture, country folk art, and fine art combine with patterns

and colors that never overwhelm. All add a richness and decorative versatility to the house.

"I like to decorate small rooms," Miriam says. "They're easy to fill and I like having lots of pretty things to look at everywhere." Her sense of style is imaginative and intimately hers. There is nothing pretentious or flashy in sight; each detail contributes to the overall atmosphere that balances respect for tradition with a designer's feel for fashion. Fresh flowers from the garden and the farm cart in town add color and scent to the rooms all summer long.

While the hallway has a relaxed country feeling, the living room is more formal, with an Old World elegance. No simple modern chairs, no unadorned floors, and not a single slipcover in sight. The luxurious tone comes from rich fabrics, marble and woods, as well as soft pastel colors.

The dining room was once the keeping room. Cooking was done in the fireplace and the built-in oven. Wide floorboards in this room have been painted deep red. Early islanders often used muted earth-tone paint colors on their walls. In this room, deep red and green emphasize the historic details: uneven transom doors, built-in fireplace shelves, wood wainscoting, and a concealed wine cupboard under the stairs.

Off the dining room is the true sitting room, with the homey clutter of comfortable furniture, a television, decorative pillows, pink geraniums in Nantucket lightship baskets, vases of cut flowers, books piled everywhere, and tables covered with family photos and favorite mementos. This room is a happy blend reflecting the comfortable living so

often found in English country homes.

French doors lead from the sitting room out to the patio. As the house is only a few doors from the center of town and surrounded by other houses, outdoor plantings have been carefully tended to provide shade-dappled sunlight and privacy, creating a world unto its own. Geraniums and pink impatiens fill the corners and borders around a stone edging; the hill that rises beyond the brick areas is covered with green ivy and pachysandra.

Miriam and Sonny enjoy many dinners in this tranquil setting. Wrought-iron chairs topped with lavender seats surround the table. When entertaining, Miriam sets her table with the same devotion she gives everything else. She puts antique linen from her vintage collection over a pink moiré table skirt, then mixes napkins and uses different sets of china until she finds a combination she likes. Add to this a bouquet of flowers that she put together on a moment's notice and you have the perfect setting.

Far left: An eighteenth-century Pennsylvania corner cupboard in the dining room has its original finish.
Above, right: An old-fashioned marble sink is the dominant feature in the downstairs bathroom. A niche in the wall holds a collection of interesting glass perfume bottles.
Top: Ursula, the family pet, sprawls in the sunlight coming through the front door.
Above: South-seas floral pillows work well with the raspberry-pink pineapple fabric on the sofa and the pink and green taffeta fabric of the curtains and wing chair. Majolica plates frame the carved pine mirror, with its gracefully curved scallop top. Family photographs fill the tables next to the sofa. Miriam's favorite picture of her husband is one in which he looks like a matinee idol, and next to it is his favorite of her, taken at a charity ball, looking elegant and sleek in a strapless gown.

LILY
STREET
COTTAGE

At one time this little cottage at 13 Lily Street was a Nantucket pots-and-pans shop. It was built in 1886, the same year The Sea Cliff Inn was erected. In March of that year the temperature reached two below zero and the steamer was frozen out of the harbor from February 28 to March 13. Two whales were captured off Tuckernuck in April.

The present owner of the house, Charles Douglas, finds the little cottage, with its diamond-paned windows, inviting front porch, and manicured yard, as charming and efficient as any small home could be.

The front door opens directly into the living room. One expects the space to be cramped, but it isn't. The ceiling starts out low for a few feet, providing a cozy, intimate feeling. Then, surprisingly, the ceiling lifts one and a half stories to the rafters where there's a second-floor sleeping loft, and the room is suddenly quite spacious. And there's another surprise. The room isn't dark and quaint. The walls and ceiling are painted bright white and there's a light and airy floral print on the curtains.

Living in a small space is an art. It takes imagination and skill to create traditional comfort without overcrowding. The furniture here is anything but precious. The ample loveseat and built-in sofa with plump cushions are covered with blue-and-white ticking. An overstuffed armchair and wonderful bamboo-frame chair complete the arrangement around the coffee table. A mix of antique pieces with contemporary accessories and selected paintings make this home quite stylish. Charles Douglas spends most of his summers here. In the off-season he uses the house for long weekends. A wood-burning stove makes the place warm and inviting.

Above: The little cottage on Lily Street was once the pots-and-pans shop. Blue flowering-hydrangea bushes fill the front and side areas just inside the neatly capped fence surrounding the property.
Right: The kitchen is compact and cleverly efficient. Blue placemats and china interplay with the color of the hydrangeas just outside the window.

Left: Pretty fabrics, white walls, and carefully arranged paintings add up to a charming, light, and airy room. The house is always filled with fresh-cut flowers from the garden.

Above and bottom left: A back door leads to what can only be described as a delightful English cottage garden. The flower beds bordering the yard and along the fence are vibrant with poppies, lilies, daisies, and old farmhouse hollyhocks that match the old-fashioned charm of the garden and cottage.

Bottom right: A collection of old doorstops leads the eye up the winding stairs to the loft bedroom.

THERE ONCE WAS A COBBLER'S SHOP

In the 1700s, there was a tiny one-room cobbler's shop on Orange Street. Since the population of Nantucket was nearly five thousand, it must have been a busy place. Though the population is almost double that today, it's interesting that there's no shoemaker on Nantucket. Residents must take their shoes across the bay to Hyannis for repair.

Eventually, the shop was converted into a delightful one-room house that changed hands many times. A small dormer bedroom with bay window was added by the present owner. Surprisingly, the original cobbler's bench, with all his tools intact, has remained in the house over the years and is now used as an end table. The front deck, which extends the living space all summer long, is another new addition.

This house is home to Ray Dawson for six months of the year. Situated in the historic district of town, the location is convenient, yet private. The little house sits sideways on the property behind another building. Surrounded by full bushes, flowering plants, and mature trees,

it is so secluded that you'd never know it was there. When invited for tea, you simply step off the busy street onto the brick walkway, lift the latch to the gate, follow the path through the yard to the steps that lead up to the deck, open the screen door, and you're there.

Ray's inventive decorating is the most interesting thing about this house. He has covered every wall with a collection of small paintings and prints by Nantucket artists.

Nantucket has always been an art colony, attracting talented people from all over the world. Island galleries abound. Old South Wharf, along the harbor area, has a long tradition as an artist's row. A visit to Ray's house is a fascinating excursion into the social history of Nantucket artists from as far back as most current residents can remember. It always sparks discussions about how things used to be on Nantucket. "Remember when so-and-so used to show at the Kenneth Taylor Gallery?" or, "Whatever happened to so-and-so?—I always liked going to her gallery."

Above: An early cobbler's shop was converted to a charming house. Nestled between mature hedges and trees, this private aerie is located in the heart of the Nantucket historic district. Right: Ray likes to collect the work of his artist friends who live or have lived on the island.

Far left: One wall of the room is devoted to the work of Nantucket artist Polly Bushong. To the right, a Donn Russell work hangs on the bathroom door.

Left: Impatiens surround a whale sculpture in the garden.

Above: Miniature Nantucket lightship baskets line a windowsill. The table holds a malachite-and-ivory boat model and chess set, as well as other malachite carvings that Ray purchased at the annual Nantucket antique show to add to his collection.

THE OLD GARDNER HOUSE, 1751

This little whale house on Broadway in the village of 'Sconset has remained in the same family since it was first built in 1751, except for a brief time when it was owned by the Nantucket Historical Society and operated as the 'Sconset library. The back of the house faces the water on Front Street and there is nothing between it and Spain. As with most of these houses, the back was originally the front.

Because it doesn't follow the usual layout of rooms, or appear constructed in the same way as the other whale houses in the village, it is believed that the Gardner House was actually built later than the date on its façade. The size of the great room, eleven-by-seventeen feet, is one clue, as is the arrangement of the three bedrooms (one is now a bath) on the first floor. Studies indicate that these neatly balanced rooms, exactly the same size, followed the style of houses with "warts," which came later.

No matter; every generation to descend from the Gardner family has unstintingly preserved this

house as a tribute to Nantucket history. Nancy and Peter Rodts (her paternal grandmother was a Gardner) and their five children spend every summer here, as will their grandchildren and their grandchildren's children.

It must be an incredible experience for Nancy to imagine, as she goes about the business of everyday living, her great-great-grandmother doing the very same tasks when she lived in the house almost two hundred and fifty years ago. And while the house is tilting to one side, it's amazing to realize that *anything* built that long ago could still be standing and sheltering a family today. Even more incredible is the fact that the house can accommodate a modern family of seven, although Nancy did show us that the washer is in the pantry and a dryer is neatly concealed beneath the cabinets.

This is summer living at its best. Kick off your shoes, race down to the beach, and at night gather for a simple meal around the kitchen table. This house represents a break

Top: A little whale house in 'Sconset has remained in one family for over two hundred years.
Above: Ribbons tie back the curtains so that the blue hydrangeas in the yard can be enjoyed from the kitchen.
Right: Personal details abound in the house. The blue trim and the Nantucket lightship baskets filled with hydrangeas are Nancy's touches. The needlepoint illustration of the house over the top of the mirror frame is one of her daughter Heather's creations. Forrest Rodts, a son, is an artist, and his paintings of Nantucket subjects are right at home here.

from the stresses and strains of a more complicated world and the Rodts are diligent about keeping it this way.

The great room, as the living room was called, contains an entry and one of those large fireplaces found in early homes. Used at one time for heating and cooking, it was later boarded up by a previous resident. When Nancy and Pete moved in, they opened up the fireplace and uncovered the kettle and cooking utensils just as they had been left, probably after the evening meal many, many years ago. Behind the chimney is a steep stairway to the second floor, used as a sleeping dormitory. When you're in this house it seems perfectly natural to expect Captain Gardner to walk through the front door and set himself down in his rocker by the fire.

Left: The great fireplace was once boarded up. When Nancy and Peter Rodts moved in, they uncovered it, finding old cooking utensils and a kettle left inside.
Above: A window in the great room faces the ocean. The postage-stamp backyard was once the front yard. The Rodts enjoy this special view as well as the convenience of living in the heart of the village.

The Old Gardner House
Built in 1751

Left: The kitchen is comprised of two areas, one for cooking and another for eating and socializing. Every meal here is an aesthetic experience, for the double windows over the table face the ocean. Pink geraniums and a picket fence frame this unmatched natural "painting". Above: A sign on the front of the house tells passersby of its history.
Right: The kitchen has not changed in two-hundred-and-fifty years. A picture on the wall portrays Captain Gardner and friend sitting by the stove in this room many years ago. Nancy's blue-and-white curtains might have been just as appropriate then as they are today.

A COUNTRY HOME IN 'SCONSET

When the owners first set eyes on this unpretentious little house, they must have had a great deal of courage and vision. Made up of interconnecting little rooms, the house lacked space, light, and interest, but the owners liked the property and felt they could restructure the house to fit their needs.

A bathroom in the middle of the house posed the first problem. The owners thought they'd just move this to create a master bath, then do the remodeling a little at a time. Instead they decided to gut the entire structure. What followed was a massive restoration that produced one charming and spacious living area.

It was necessary to remove and shift interior walls, rearranging the space to yield new possibilities. Low ceilings were lifted to create height and new rafters were left exposed. Each area opens to another with a different angle to the ceiling, making the small house seem surprisingly larger than it is.

The newly created living area is open from the front door to the back wall of sliding French doors that lead to a tree-shaded deck. Beyond is an unobstructed view of nature. Encompassed in the space is a very comfortable living room, open kitchen, and dining area. Off this main room is a study and bath that converts to a guest room; next to it is the charming master bedroom and the bathroom that started the whole renovation process.

Before starting the interior design, the couple spoke to their friend, Hazel Priest Korper, a well-known design consultant. Indeed, now that the job is finished, the owners credit Hazel's sensitivity to the island, inherent good taste, and years of experience for its success and appealing style. The rooms have a sophisticated country look that is uncontrived and beguiling.

Everything is light and airy. Dried flowers hang from rafters and baskets hold necessities within easy reach. Gentle colors and carefully chosen accessories work well with the scrubbed pine pieces, (like the corner cupboard that houses the VCR), floral needlepoint rugs, antique furniture, and Nantucket artifacts.

Above: An old pine cabinet fills a wall between the living and dining rooms. Nantucket art, a pinecone wreath, a primitive wood block, and an early framed document are arranged on the wall.
Right: French doors lead from the dining area to a tree-shaded deck. Deep-rose needlepoint chairs accent the colors in the floral fabrics. Island flowers grace the family-sized pine table where meals are a pleasant experience.
Overleaf: The interior of the house was completely gutted and ceilings were lifted to create an open floor plan.

Left: In the master bedroom, a willow head-board, lace tablecloths cleverly draped at the windows, antique quilts, a Nantucket lightship basket, a pine bench, and a rocker create a mood that is relaxed and comfortable.
Right: The sitting room off the living room converts easily into a guest bedroom. The tall double doors open wide to make the room seem larger. The window valances were made by hanging lace-edged linen napkins on the diagonal across wooden poles.

Handcrafted touches abound. The découpage and painted screen adds just the right amount of visual separation between the kitchen and the living room. Diana "Dolly" Hancock added her artistry here. Raised in Surrey, England, she is a graduate of The Roger Newton School of Decorative Finishes in Chelsea, England. Now living in Cabbagetown, Toronto, Canada, she visits Nantucket in the summer and has lent her talents to many of the island homes.

Beyond the kitchen, the dining area incorporates a sofa and piano. Everything benefits from the pretty tones of pink. A loosely arranged bouquet of island flowers is perfect in these surroundings. A round pine table pulls to the center of the room when the family gathers or guests arrive. The deck extends the living space from spring through Nantucket's delicious Indian summer. All the cushions are covered in faded red canvas, a tribute to the popular slacks locally called "Nantucket reds."

WINDOW BOXES

Window boxes are ubiquitous on Nantucket. You'll find them on grand homes, little cottages, and almost every storefront. And while the buildings might be grey and somber, the window boxes are bursting with color. From spring through summer, window boxes brim with geraniums, petunias, and impatiens.

THE PENCE SCHOOL

Back in 1799 there was a street called Crown Court. It was a little side street in the center of town and for some unknown reason around 1858 became Quince Street. Of special interest on this street is a building at number 8, once a Quaker schoolhouse moved here from Fair Street.

No one knows exactly when The Pence School became a private home, but there have been many owners, artists among them, and restoration work has been sensitively done to preserve the character and integrity of the little schoolhouse.

When Dr. Thomas Sollas, Jr. asked his wife Ann what she'd like for an important wedding anniversary gift, she didn't hesitate for a minute. "A house on Nantucket Island," was her response. It didn't take them long to find and fall in love with the little gem of a schoolhouse.

The house was in splendid shape when the Sollases purchased it, but with just one bedroom, it was too tiny for their needs. They first thought to add a bedroom off to the

side where the deck now stands. Because the building is so close to its neighbors on either side, The Nantucket Historic District Commission would not grant permission to expand in this direction. The only solution was to gain room at the top.

With the help of island architect Chris Holland, the new plan included raising the roof for the addition of a master bedroom and bath, as well as a study for Tom. To get to this level, a little jog was cleverly added at the top of the existing stairway. A few steps take you up to the new suite.

The first floor of the schoolhouse is divided into a living room and kitchen. The main room is one-and-a-half stories high and sunlight streams through the tall windows on either side of the massive cobblestone fireplace. The floor in front of the fireplace lists unevenly. It's appropriate to the age and charm of the house.

Much of the original restoration work was done by The Weatherhill Restoration Company, a group of skilled preservationists who dismantle and save endangered old houses. They were able to salvage many of

Above: This converted one-room schoolhouse is located on a side street in the heart of town. Right: The faux-finished mirror above the massive cobblestone fireplace was created at The Isabel O'Neil Studio. Tom's fishing rods in the corner, furniture that once belonged to his family, photographs on the tables, and books piled everywhere give the room a lived-in feeling. The ship model, "Sea Wind," on the coffee table is by island craftsman Grey Colin.

Left: A scrubbed-pine corner cupboard, actually the top of a two-piece unit, cleverly conceals the refrigerator in the kitchen.
Right: Vintage lace covers the bed in the master bedroom. And yes, that is a bear on top of the bed. The birch chairs and headboard were made to order from Ann's design and add a rustic touch. The painting of daisies—Ann's favorite flowers—on the wall by the stairs is by local artist Mary Grey.

the old pine floorboards that needed replacement and recycle them as wainscoting around the walls.

It's as though this house were waiting for Tom and Ann to fill it with family treasures. Many of the antiques belonged to Tom's family for generations and were brought here from the couple's home in Bay-head, New Jersey. Early American and European furniture of just the right proportion, comfortable uphol-stered sofas and chairs, folk and fine art live in perfect harmony. The ship model "Sea Wind" on the coffee table is by island craftsman Grey Co-lin. Ann's collection of vintage teddy bears is arranged here and there, adding a note of lightheartedness throughout the house.

An impressive collection of "Wool-ies" lines the stairway wall. Of all the maritime arts, these embroi-dered ship portraits have remained the least known. Thought to have originated in Britain in the 1840s, no one knows for sure who made them. It's believed that, much like scrimshaw, this craft was created by sailors seeking ways to relieve

Left: A narrow stairway leads from the living room to the guest bedroom, then up a few more steps to a loft-like master bedroom. The sailboat and red hull were purchased at the Forager House Collections.
Right: A ship model, "Beetle Whaleboat," was made by island craftsman Grey Colin.
Below: When the roof was raised, the old bedroom became a spacious guest room with a high ceiling. No longer a little cubby tucked under the eaves, this is a room to book for a serious week of pampering oneself. Folk toys, teddy bears, and books would make any guest feel welcome. The miniature paintings come from Carolyn Walsh's Sailor's Valentine Gallery.

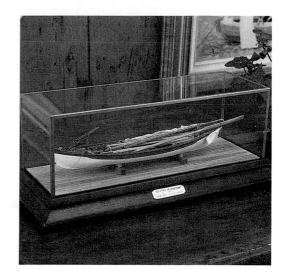

boredom and fill their leisure hours at sea.

There's nothing more traditional in a Nantucket home than an arrangement of freshly cut flowers. They bring the pleasure of the unexpected and give new life to the surroundings. The country baskets in the living room and the kitchen are the creations of Michael Molinar and Jack Bangs from Flowers at The Boarding House, whose artistry is appreciated by discerning home owners all summer long. The simple and natural approach they bring to their work is fresh and uncomplicated in the Nantucket tradition, and their arrangements look as though they have made the·transition from garden to tabletop with the greatest of ease.

The front door to the house is oversized and quite heavy. It's not hard to imagine small school children piling through to the tiny vestibule, now the front hallway. Pegs line the only wall area and everyone hangs their belongings here, just as the children might have years ago when they attended the Pence School. A

Left: "Woolies" lining the stairway are pictures made by using colorful wool, linen, cotton, and silk to fill in a simple outline of the subject drawn onto a background cloth. These simple, hand-stitched portraits can be found in major maritime museums and folk art collections, but most remain in private homes in Great Britain and the United States, where they have been passed down through families.

Right: The English pine table in the kitchen came from Ann's now-closed antique shop in Bayhead, New Jersey. The rolling pin is a local antique from the Forager House Collection. It belongs to the man of the house, who also happens to be the head cook. A Scandinavian-style closet bed conceals appliances underneath. Blue-and-white homespun fabric is a country favorite, and is repeated on the chair cushions. The painting is by an artist friend of Ann's, Mary Richardson.

doorway leads from here straight ahead to the kitchen.

This room has the flair of a Scandinavian cottage kitchen inspired by the paintings of Carl Larsson. There are all sorts of architectural details: exposed beams, wide pine floorboards, and enormous wood-framed windows. A Norwegian-inspired, built-in closet bed at one end of the room is a unique feature of the country kitchen. The natural wood tones are an essential ingredient in the room's warmth and appeal.

ROOTED
IN FAMILY
TRADITION

West Chester Street is probably the oldest road on the island. The first Meeting House, the Town House, and other buildings owned by Nantucket's earliest settlers were located here in old Sherburne, outside present limits of the town. The house at 9 West Chester Street was built sometime between 1790 and 1800 and was owned by one family until well-known artist Sybil Graham Goldsmith bought it.

A typical Nantucket dwelling with two and a half stories, here each generation has contributed to its current look. "Each family added or took away what suited their needs, mostly doorways," Sybil told a couple who had come by to make arrangements for the portrait of their children. "The medallion, for example, was added to the living-room ceiling during the Victorian era."

One of the nice things about living in an old house is discovering its individuality and eccentricities. It might be a quirky door, a delightful little alcove, or early architectural details. This house, while altered, has kept its historic character. Perhaps this is

Top left: Built in the late eighteenth century, this house is on Nantucket's oldest street.
Left: A model of buildings and a boat pier made of cedar shakes by a retired sea captain sit atop an English box probably owned by an early craftsman.
Above: There are gardens of lush plantings on different levels around the property.
Right: The Sheraton table between the two front windows in the living room was made in 1735. It is made of plum-pudding mahogany inlaid with rosewood and satinwood. To the left are a rare mahogany plant stand and a chair that belonged to Sybil's father.

why no one can resist asking for a tour of the house.

The interior is filled with family treasures and, like the house, everything is authentic. "I can remember acquiring every single thing in the house," Sybil explains.

Everything here has a personal history, giving it meaning. Sybil is comfortable surrounded by inherited pieces that evoke fond memories, keeping alive the events and people that matter and have contributed to the quality of her life. Nothing was purchased because it was fashionable. There is a purpose to it all.

The sun comes through the crisp white eyelet curtains into the peach-colored parlor and warms the memento-filled room. "This was my father's chair," Sybil says, lovingly sliding a hand over the worn soft wood on the arms of a wing chair. "Father used to have all the answers to problems. This is where I sit when I have something special to think about."

It's both stimulating and restful here, because Sybil has the artist's ability to arrange objects so they

stand on their own, yet relate harmoniously to one another. Each area of a room or a tabletop is interesting to the casual observer, but for the owner, goes beyond the aesthetically pleasing.

There's a glassed-in addition to the living room. It is from this cheerful room that Sybil gets the best view of the rest of the house and where so much of what delights her is displayed.

Though many generations of one family lived here before Sybil and her family, the Graham Goldsmith presence is very much part of it now. Sybil has incorporated the intertwining lives of her family and friends through her collections and mementos, framed newspaper clippings, photographs, war records, a collage of medals, art, and American folk art.

Sometimes when you're in a house dating back so far, you imagine what it might have been like to live here then. But this isn't the case in Sybil's house, because it's so up-to-date in many regards. Perhaps it's the artist's paintings which fill the

Far left: The skillfully crafted brick fireplace wall adds a special warmth to the room. The flag was made secretly in Sybil's father's office in Brussels during World War I. It was waved out the window when American troops came in at the end of the war. Tony Sarg marionnettes hang from the knobs of an English tool box. A boys' dollhouse, complete with elevator, is a replica of the Graham Warehouse—the family business. The old clock came from her family's summer house.

Above, left: Bookshelves line the walls in the sunroom. The top shelf is crammed with judiciously arranged model furniture pieces and rare "whimsies". A saleman's sample desk from Portsmouth, New Hampshire, holds tiny lightship baskets.

Above, center: A Victorian doll sits on a chair next to a glass case filled with an assortment of costumed dolls.

Above: Summer flowers in the dining room come from the gardens around the house. Portraits of her sons that Sybil painted hang on either side of the window. The old-fashioned highchair with the rag doll adds a lighthearted note.

Left and right: In the light-filled country kitchen, baskets hang from the rafters, and crocks and boxes are all within reach. The worn pine table is filled with the fresh vegetables just brought back from the farm cart and it's here that Sybil also arranges cut flowers from the garden.

walls, that give the rooms their vitality. There must be thousands of her paintings all over the island, for this prolific and versatile painter's work has always been sought after. The people who come to commission portraits of their children these days were once the children whose portraits Sybil painted years ago. Her interpretations of the natural environment of the island grace homes here, off island, and abroad, where she once maintained a studio. A Sybil Goldsmith show at The Main Street Gallery is always popular.

When Sybil bought the house over twenty years ago, her son, Graham, was an architectural student studying under Louis Kahn, a renowned architect. Sybil needed a studio and Graham undertook the problem as a design project. "He asked me what I wanted in a studio," she says, "and I answered, 'I want a grown-up playhouse.'" What she got was a delightful environment that looks like a treehouse from the outside, with rough-hewn wood and tiny peepholes for windows here and there.

The studio is filled with color and energy and light and one is instantly drawn into another environment, the world of the artist. Sybil has no set times when she works, but it is obvious from the sheer amount of paintings in the studio, and the number of paintings one sees in Nantucket homes, that this lady is a prolific painter.

Above, right: A niche houses a collection of stoneware. Made since the 1700s in many parts of the United States, stoneware is a valued collectible. Framed family photographs fill a narrow wall to the left.
Right: The tabletop arrangement in the living room includes a black madonna from Barcelona. A Queen Elizabeth doll wears an exquisite beaded dress and holds leather gloves in one hand and a fan in the other. Her two petticoats and lace pantaloons are in perfect condition. A book of old Godey prints lies open on the table.
Center right: The front-hall alcove is arranged by the artist as if for a still-life painting.
Far right: The studio was designed by Sybil's son, Graham Goldsmith. Clever window controls enable Sybil to adjust light. A stairway to the left leads to a balcony and a little doorway with a peephole window.

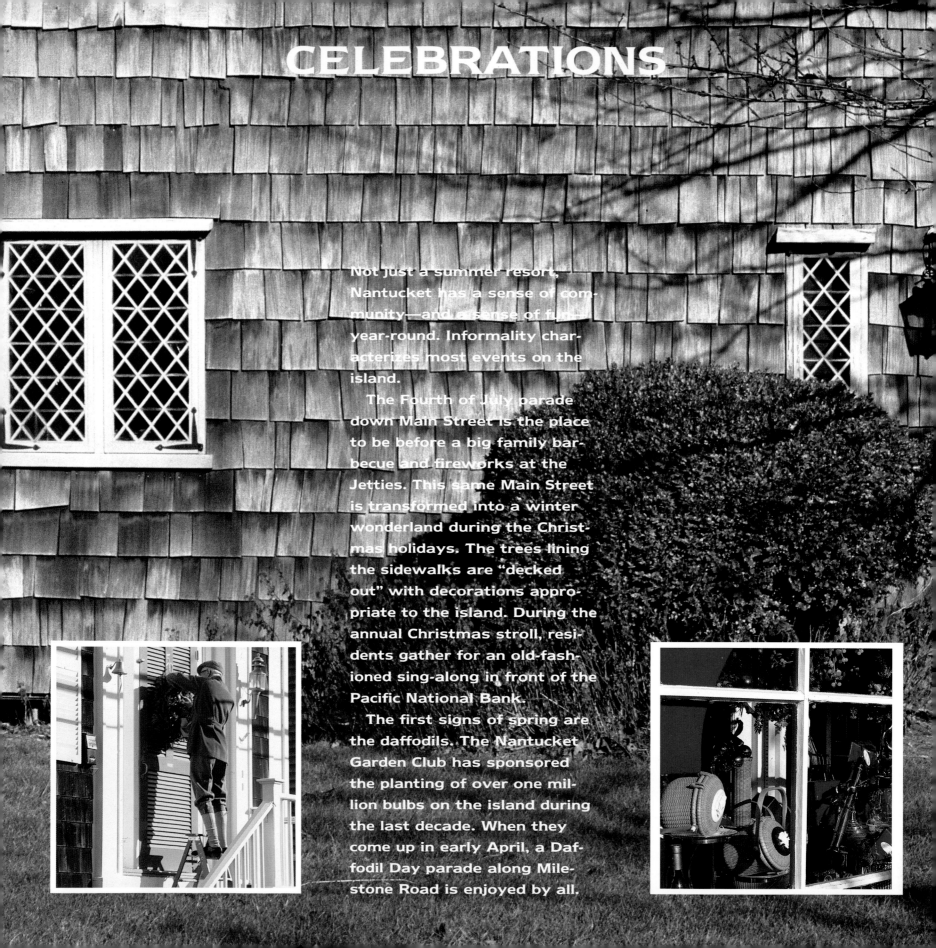

CELEBRATIONS

Not just a summer resort, Nantucket has a sense of community—and a sense of fun—year-round. Informality characterizes most events on the island.

The Fourth of July parade down Main Street is the place to be before a big family barbecue and fireworks at the Jetties. This same Main Street is transformed into a winter wonderland during the Christmas holidays. The trees lining the sidewalks are "decked out" with decorations appropriate to the island. During the annual Christmas stroll, residents gather for an old-fashioned sing-along in front of the Pacific National Bank.

The first signs of spring are the daffodils. The Nantucket Garden Club has sponsored the planting of over one million bulbs on the island during the last decade. When they come up in early April, a Daffodil Day parade along Milestone Road is enjoyed by all.

A COUNTRY RETREAT IN TOWN

The gambrel-roof house at 30 Hussey Street sits diagonally on the road as it curves away from town. It was built in 1772 by Grondell Gardner, whose father, Abel, owned the land it was situated on, as well as the house across the street, known as the Abel Gardner Mansion House. It passed title only five times in the last two hundred years, often within the same family. Other than the addition of a family room and workroom, not much changed it until it was sold in 1982 to its present owners.

The new owners undertook a major restoration. While the entire house was renovated, the owners took great care to preserve its flavor, carefully saving elements in good condition and improving what could be made better.

Today, the house is bright and cheerful. The owners enjoy the house all summer and find it equally comfortable as a weekend retreat in the off-season.

The double-pitched, half-gambrel roof is one of the unusual features of this house. Of English origin, it never really became popular in this country, so there are very few examples; only eight exist on Nantucket. This house has one and a half stories. The present dormers were added in the 1890s.

The layout of the house has remained basically intact, with a center stairway and two rooms off to each side. One front room serves as a living room, the other a study. One of the former owners laid new flooring which deteriorated with time. The owners removed these floors and discovered the original pine floorboards beneath. These were badly damaged, but enough of the old wood was salvageable for use in other parts of the house. The new kitchen was built from these old floorboards. Enough was left over for most of the moldings and beams, which contribute greatly to the character of the house and reflect the sound sensibility brought to the restoration work.

In back of the study there is a sitting room. This is a playful area that the owner calls her ET, or entertainment room. It houses a collection of

Above: A gambrel-roof house is one of only eight on Nantucket.
Right: The primitive hooked rug hanging in the dining room is quite appropriate. Befitting the times, it's an illustration of an "unliberated" couple preparing for dinner.

toys and old children's books that belonged to one of the earliest families who lived here. They are quite rare and have been artfully arranged to be appreciated for their interest and authenticity, mixing well with the newer things on the tables and shelves over the country sofa.

But there is more to the downstairs of the house. At the back, an old-fashioned extension was added about forty or fifty years ago. It was an ugly addition that included a family room and a workroom that housed the furnace. This area was completely stripped away and transformed into what is now the heart of the house, a suite of rooms: a family room and kitchen, as well as a master bedroom and bath.

The family room is open to the dining and ET room. The tiled floor is on a slightly lower level, just one step down, so you know you're entering another dimension. This room reflects the personal style of the owners, complete with all sorts of treasures found in island antique stores, at local auctions, and culled during their many trips around the world. Creative in their approach to living, the owners are always on the lookout for unusual or interesting items for their homes here and in New York City. This is where they live and entertain all summer long. There are windows all around the room, making it part of the outdoors. The French doors open to a secluded patio surrounded by foliage. The garden is surprisingly peaceful and private, even though the house is situated right in the heart of this historic town. The new family room makes the most of the lovely setting.

Left: The master bedroom opens onto the patio. There's a large Chinese-export trunk inscribed "Nantucket" at the foot of the pencil-post bed.
Above: The dining room is elegant in its simplicity. The owners' approach to country decorating is very much in tune with Shaker aesthetics—spare and strongly graphic. A Danish pine table and milk-painted chairs are offset against white plaster walls. Irregular paneling on one wall and wooden beams warm the room. The back stairway was never changed and dates to the 1700s.
Right: An eyelet umbrella with a beautifully carved ivory handle hangs in the family room. The side table with its weathered blue paint was once a butter churn and the painted blue chest in front of the sofa is a rare Nantucket antique. It's signed and dated inside "Folger 1821." The wooden carved box on the floor to the left is a Swedish dowry box and the large bolster on the sofa was made from a rag rug.

Left: There is a joyful mix of quilts and floral fabrics on the white iron bed and wicker rocker in one of the guest bedrooms.

Above: An extra bedroom was made into a large bathroom. The original deep-soaking tub under the treetop windows gives the bathroom a sense of old-fashioned luxury.

Right: Some of the furniture in the family room came with the house and dates back to the earliest owners. The dough trough in front of the sofa was purchased at a local auction and probably came from an early Nantucket home. The Danish rag rug is quite old, as are the other scatter rugs throughout the house. Tapestry and quilted pillows are right at home here, as is Cato, a Himalayan cat.

ON HITHER CREEK

It's almost dusk. The road to Madaket, a village at the western tip of the island, curves gracefully as it leaves town. Just over a crest, the sky bursts across the horizon in streaks of pink, purple, and fiery yellow as the sun begins its final descent. At every dip and curve of the road the view changes.

Back in the early 1600s, there were nine First Purchasers of the island of Nantucket. In the fall of 1659, Thomas Macy and his wife were the first to arrive. They chose to settle in Madaket. However, while Madaket, which means "sandy soil," was a fine area for fishing, it proved too harsh for planting. The following year, sixty settlers moved inland between Capaum and Hummock Pond.

In the beginning, the Indians taught the whites how to whale. The settlers built shacks and then houses near the shore. Madaket is still known as a fishing village and residents have bought houses here to vacation and take advantage of the fishing and boating from Madaket Harbor and Hither Creek.

Things have remained pretty much the way they always have been here. In the winter, the harbor is filled with boats owned by local residents who scallop for a living.

When Carol and Karl Lindquist first bought their house, friends thought they were crazy. It was a plain and nondescript structure, undistinguished and run-down. But it wasn't the house that interested them so much as the fact that it was situated right on Hither Creek. The Lindquists knew from past experience that with a little imagination they could turn a tired, outmoded house into a waterfront gem.

Karl Lindquist grew up on Nantucket. As a young boy he learned to sail and fish, and though he moved away after college, his career as a teacher allowed him summers in Madaket, returning to his childhood pleasures. When he retired from teaching, he moved back to Nantucket and started a new career renovating houses. So it was with a sense of the place that the Lindquists set out to capture the spirit of old Madaket when they reno-

Top: The house overlooks Hither Creek in Madaket. Its renovation was influenced by the boathouses and lifesaving stations on Nantucket.
Above: The dining table is set for afternoon tea. A cake was baked by neighbor Bonnie Ray for an anniversary celebration. Light pours in from the cupola above, setting the proper mood.
Right: This country kitchen has an international flavor; many of its furnishings were purchased by the owners while abroad. All the appliances, including the Paul Bocuse French restaurant stove, line one wall. The decorative tiles above the stove came from a *brocante* in Spain. The back doors came from a rectory. The checkerboard floor was created using white ceramic tile and grey slate.

Left: A model of a Bequia whale boat is on display under a painting by local artist John Austin.

Right: A French fisherman's workbasket, found in Normandy, holds wood next to the living-room fireplace. A willow trunk that serves as a coffee table was found in a French ship's chandlery. The half model of a Bahamian sailing dinghy was brought back from a sailing trip. Carol devised the candlesticks from wooden spools and glass globes found in the local Hospital Thrift Shop, a regular haunt closer to home.

Overleaf: The first floor, once comprised of many small rooms, was gutted and opened up to create a living room that takes advantage of the waterfront views. The melon basket next to the sofa was a wedding gift from Gretchen Anderson, a well-known local basketmaker. Her classic, twisted seagrass and reed baskets are in great demand on the island. Yella, the family pet, was a stray found on a boat dock in Greece.

vated this house.

"I knew that once we'd gutted the house we could make it look like the old lifesaving stations on Nantucket," Karl explains.

Karl's knowledge of local history and building traditions and Carol's background in interior design proved invaluable as they approached the project with very definite design ideas. The challenge was to create a house that would complement the area and take advantage of the water views.

While the nature of the remodeling was fairly conventional, involving the taking down of walls to create one large room, the results are anything but ordinary. When you walk into the house it seems more like you've stepped outside it.

The double glass doors on the water side of the house and the front windows almost touching the floor are the essence of summertime living. No curtains obstruct the views, which are as important to the rooms as the interior furnishings. Walls are painted perfectly white, the pickled oak floors are a pale seashell pink.

Through the doors, porches wrap around three sides of the house. While the owners wanted a huge front porch, they were not allowed to build one because of stringent zoning laws. Carol says, "Sometimes a limitation can be turned into an advantage, and that's just what happened. We ended up with a narrow porch that runs around the house like a passageway on a ship's deck. It's quite nautical, and anchors the house to the landscape."

The interior of the house reflects more than an association with the water and boating. Everywhere you turn it's filled with found treasures. Carol and Karl share a love for traveling and delight in finding things off the beaten track. "We hunt for bargains in little antique shops," Carol says. "There is a name for these shops in France, which is *brocante*. It means a little better than a secondhand shop. Actually, this is where I find the most interesting country accessories."

This adventurous approach to collecting is evident in the way they've furnished their Madaket home. Everything tells a story. Combined with this eclectic mix are nautical things and Nantucket memorablia. Lots of the objects came from Carol's father's boat.

Bronze eye straps used for threading line on boats were added as door pulls on the cabinets in the country kitchen. Carol says that, when used judiciously, nautical touches such as these can be quite sophisticated. Nothing was done by accident here, but rather by design.

Left: The steep back stairway is typical of Nantucket houses. In keeping with a nautical theme, beaded pine walls were painted white. A Swedish handwoven runner carpets the stair treads, and heavy boat line, knotted through brass eye straps and rings, creates the handrail. Brass bulkhead lights illuminate the way. A framed Nantucket Chamber of Commerce "Rules of Conduct" hangs on one wall. On the other, one finds private signal flags of Nantucket whaling merchants. The carved walking sticks were found at country fairs on the south coast of England. Casually arranged field flowers are a Nantucket tradition, as is the sight of a yellow slicker and waders at the back door.

Above: The sitting room was once a downstairs bedroom and is now an ell open to the living room.

Right: Among the collectibles on display are four baskets made by French itinerant basketmakers, three by Nantucket crafter Cynthia Young, and three by Carol Lindquist. One basket was woven of willow from the tree under which the owners were married at Île au Thon, France. French pewter measures and a collection of antique alarm clocks complete the arrangement.

NANTUCKET GREY

The harmony of Nantucket is due in part to the soft, silver grey, weathered shingles on most of the houses and town buildings. When the fog rolls in over the town, as it frequently does, the entire island takes on a soft, grey, hazy look. The only distracting elements are the white trims and an occassional black, deep red, or green door. The greyness favored by the Quakers went along with their belief that a house should be basic and functional, but never adorned.

The Nantucket Historic District Commission meets regularly to hear requests for various building, remodeling, or repair plans for island dwellings. These townspeople are charged with enforcing the visual guidelines of Nantucket's history, which extends to the paint colors used on the exteriors of the houses.

Grey is a perfect backdrop for the sunny days of summer, the New England foliage in fall, and the crisp whiteness of newly fallen snow.

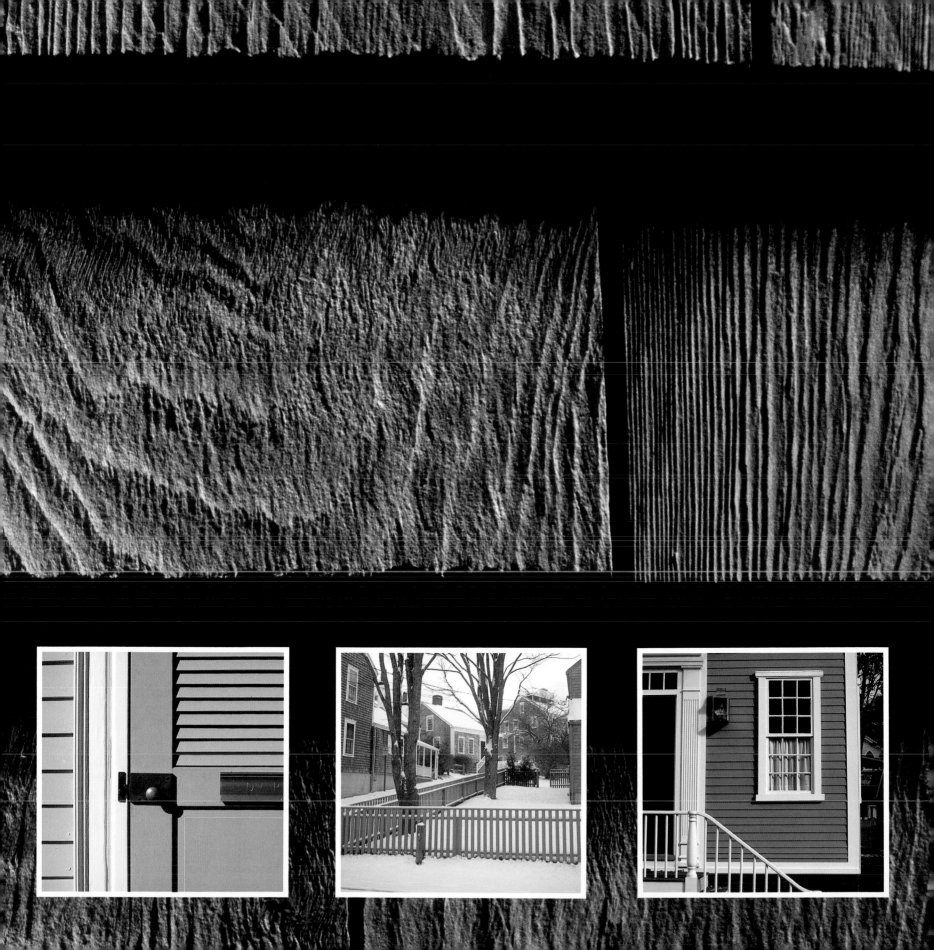

OVERLOOKING DIONIS

The beach area on the north shore, known as Dionis, was named for the wife of Tristram Coffin, an original settler of Nantucket. Many new houses have been built in this area to take advantage of the views and proximity to the water.

You see the house high on a hill before you actually reach it. Once you've traversed the winding dirt road and turned into the driveway, the view is so spectacular you know it was worth the trip. This is where Robert and Carolyn Walsh live.

As soon as you arrive, the spirit of the place takes over. It's a welcome breath of fresh air from the closeness of the town. And this is just what Robert and Carolyn wanted.

Carolyn is the owner of the Sailor's Valentine Gallery on Centre Street and finds this the perfect antidote to a long day in the bustling downtown area. An elegant little sitting room off the dining area was designed to accommodate two overstuffed chairs and ottomans. This is where they sit at the end of the day and watch the sun disappear over the water.

When Lyn called Gary Knight to help decorate the house, the two immediately saw eye to eye. The family room is on a lower level than the rest of the house and it responds to everyone's needs.

In keeping with Gary's sensitivity to the island's beauty and his sensibility about decorating with Nantucket in mind, he used the natural colors that one sees from the windows. He used the warmer colors of spring and fall. Since the couple lives here year-round, the choice of rosier tones made sense. A woven rug by Margareta Nettles picks up the peachy colors of the fabrics and pink and white tones in the fireplace brick.

The Sailor's Valentine Gallery represents American and European fine and folk artists, some from Nantucket. The house is a more informal background for the art, allowing friends, artists, and patrons to appreciate the artwork in a more intimate environment. Gary made the family room work from a design point of view. Lyn skillfully arranged the art and crafts she especially treasures.

Above: The house sits on a high ridge overlooking the ocean.
Right: A painting by Clementine Hunter, one of this country's best-known folk artists, hangs over the mantel. The painted rooster is by Marvin Finn, a Kentucky "outsider artist." This term is new for more primitive folk artists who work or live "outside" the mainstream. The clay rooster at the left is an example of Mississippi mud art.
Overleaf: The dining room has a sweeping view of the ocean. The vegetable bowl on the kitchen counter was made by a Nantucket Indian.

Above: Island decorator Gary Knight used the rosy colors of nature that one sees from the windows in the family room.

Right: Primarily made for utilitarian purposes, carved walking sticks by Kentucky artists are becoming recognized as primitive folk art.

Far right: The cherry cupboard in the family room once belonged to the late Billy Baldwin, a Nantucket resident and well-known interior decorator. The chair to the left was once a throne in a Scandinavian court of the late nineteenth century. The painting above the cupboard is by Steve Cull. A baleen box and sailor's valentine sit next to a lightship purse, a testament to Nantucket's maritime heritage. Sailor's valentines are made from shells set in symmetrical patterns, then mounted in single or double octagonal frames. Most were made in Barbados, which was a regular stop for returning American whalers in the nineteenth century, who brought them home to loved ones.

LIVING
WITH
FOLK ART

Madaquecham Valley is located
off Milestone Road. Driving through
the moors is indeed a spiritual experience. It's no wonder these moors
are often compared to the heaths of
Scotland. Rabbits scurry across the
path. Birds, owls, and an occasional
hawk can be seen. The road winds
and bumps, and as you begin to
wonder where it will end, the ocean
breathtakingly emerges in front of
you.

There are few houses out this
way, and the three-acre zoning affords much privacy. Richard Kemble
and George Korn live in one of the
houses only steps from the ocean.
Theirs is a remote and self-reliant
home, designed for simple living. Every room has a view of the moors
and the water beyond. The sounds
of the ocean are ever-present.

The front door leads from the living room to an open deck where the
owners and their guests often
spend lazy afternoons in the wake
of sea breezes and salty air. Out the
kitchen door to the back of the
house is the studio, where Richard
creates his much-sought-after paint-

**Top left: This house at Madaquecham has
breathtaking views of the ocean.**
Left: The view from the upstairs bathroom.
**Above: In the sitting area at the top of the
winding stairs, an arrangement of colorful
vases, bowls, and bottles line a late-nine-
teenth-century painted shelf under the sky-
light. A vinegar-grained blanket chest holds a
rare folk art paddleboat, borrowed from the
owner's shop. George likens the early hooked
rug to a Frank Stella painting.**
**Right: A painted country cupboard in the living
room is flanked by simple school chairs. An elegant ensemble of ceramic bowls by renowned
artisan Hannelore Fasciszewski and an oversized lightship basket complement a large
woodcut by Richard Kemble. A petite harpsi-
chord is tucked under the stairway that leads
up to a small loft-like sitting room overlooking
the living and dining areas.**

Left: The second-floor bedroom is deliberately stark to take advantage of the natural beauty of the view framed by the arched window. A rare, blown-glass witch's ball is silhouetted against the sky. When the window is open, the breeze gently turns the arms of the carved whirligig. Antique walking sticks are mounted on individual stands.
Right: A bucket of flowers sits in front of the potting shed before being separated into arrangements for the house. The garden along the fence is rarely bare, except for a few months in winter.

ings, prints, and collages sold through galleries on island and in Pennsylvania.

For Kemble and Korn, the house is an environment for the carefully selected folk art that is the trademark of their downtown antique shop, Forager House Collection. The unique whirligigs and old baskets are among their favorite collectibles; they fit right in with Nantucket style. "The house is a revolving gallery of sorts for the things we love," George says.

The living room, open all the way up to the rafters, has a spacious feeling. A colorful kite made by Al Hartig, known as "The Nantucket kiteman," is suspended from the high ceiling and adds to the playful scene.

A witch whirligig on a living-room table is an exceptional example of folk art by local crafter Lincoln Ceely, who lived on Nantucket from 1866 to 1950. Very few pieces of his work are left on the island. Another whirligig sits on an overhead beam waiting to catch an occasional breeze. Things move gently here.

Left: In a corner of the bedroom under the sloped roof, a painted country desk holds an unusual display of marine craft objects, including woven baskets and sailor's valentines. A ripe pear on the windowsill creates, if only for a moment, a Magrittelike image.

Above: The angles of the bedroom roof converge above a shelf in back of the bed where objects can be displayed and appreciated from time to time. The very dark and delicate basket, probably made in the late 1800s, is filled with whalebone clothespins—highly prized collectibles that were used throughout the eighteenth and nineteenth centuries on Nantucket.

Below: The living room opens to a deck and the ocean beyond. The moors and the water go on for as far as one can see.

Right: "End-of-the-day" glass lines a shelf in the sitting room. The colorful blown glass got its name for obvious reasons: At the end of a day, a glass blower created what he could by using all the leftover material from the day's output.

A WARM-HEARTED HOME

Maggie Meredith is a witty artist, poet (her new book is *Not Beyond Recall*), quiltmaker, rug hooker, inveterate collector, and all-around talented lady. She has such an infectious laugh that you know the minute you enter her house or studio that her work will be fun. Her house is literally jammed with vibrant colors, texture, shapes, and good humor. There are symbols and signs everywhere that express "love," "heart," "home," and "teddy bears," in capital letters so you will not miss them.

The house was built twenty-one years ago on Mill Hill, within sight of Nantucket's Old Mill. The Mill, here long before Maggie's house, is one of Nantucket's most outstanding buildings. Built in 1746, it is still in use, grinding corn just as it did two hundred and fifty years ago.

Little by little, the Meredith house sprouted a studio, then a guest house, and finally, a new dining room and bedroom wing. "It just keeps rambling along, like me," Maggie says with a laugh. Everywhere one turns, her special brand of

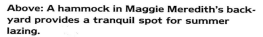

Above: A hammock in Maggie Meredith's backyard provides a tranquil spot for summer lazing.
Above, right: A geranium painting by the owner is surrounded by boxes, blocks, and figurines. An old crate mounted on the fireplace wall brims with miniature baskets.
Right: Art, quilts, hooked rugs, needlepoint, and graphic designs fill the spacious living room. A painting by Maggie's father, renowned artist Nathaniel Pousette-Dart, hangs over the sofa.

Above: One of the owner's paintings fills the wall of the dining room. A patchwork quilt, a cat cutout, a lightship basket, and a handful of posies are also on hand.
Right: The bedroom wing opens onto a sun-drenched deck filled with pots of flowers and surrounded by a multi-level garden. Colorful hooked rugs, wooden cutout cats, a patchwork quilt, and a Maggie Meredith painting attest to just how prolific this artist is.
Far right: The fireplace wall offers an arrangement of old and new elements. The cat painting, hanging between her early Nantucket samplers, is a Maggie Meredith trademark.

well-placed frivolity and good humor are in evidence, making the rooms inviting.

When you drive up the hill to the top of the driveway, you're not quite sure which way to enter. There's a door to the side, a front door, and a sign pointing the way to the studio entrance. You may pause to decide the nature of your business before proceeding, but almost everyone just walks in and yells, "Maggie, are you here?" and her voice precedes her, letting you know you're in the right place, no matter what door you've entered.

In the living room, overstuffed sofas create a seating area around the oak coffee table. Each area in the sprawling room is as comfortable and inviting as the next, but the main attraction is the art and craft work and the colors that spread generously from room to room.

The floors are covered with hooked rugs designed by Maggie, and there are patchwork quilts over the sofas and chairs. The needlepoint pillows are alive with her famous cats and sayings. Stenciled

banners attest to her love of Nantucket Island.

Nautical artifacts are combined with folk art and early American toys, vintage boxes, and favorite memorabilia. There are photographs sending out images of happy times, loving smiles, precious memories. This is a place where an adult can be a kid again.

Go to any local auction, antique fair, yard sale, or flea market and Maggie will be there looking to unearth those irresistable treasures to cart home and niche into pleasant little spaces. She knows how to pull off her uncanny predeliction for nostalgia. What might elsewhere appear as a conglomeration of interests and styles is rendered harmonious here. The house and its collections work together as an energetic whole.

The walls are covered with Maggie's own art, and that of her friends and family members. She comes by her talent naturally. Her father, Nathaniel Pousette-Dart, was a noted painter, as is her brother, Richard Pousette-Dart. Their work is also displayed throughout the house.

Far left: The pine corner cupboard display reveals Maggie's love of teddy bears. An interest in graphic design is evident in her collectibles with stenciled letters. The humorous self-sculpture of two figures at the piano was crafted by Maggie's son and daughter-in-law. He's a musician and she's a dancer.
Above: From the office, one has a clear view through the kitchen to the living room beyond. The vegetable signs were purchased at the annual Nantucket antique fair.
Left: Miniature chairs line a narrow wall in the office. The cupboard at the left houses a variety of objects that often elicit giggles.

OUR HOUSE

Below, top: The office leads into the design studio from the house. There's a guest bedroom, bath, and galley kitchen in the studio.
Below, bottom: Part of the living room is open to the second floor, creating a bit of drama where the ceiling curves.
Right: The living room is two steps up from the tiled entryway. French doors across the back of the house lead to a silver-grey deck on one level and a brick patio a few steps down.

"We want a house that is spare—the essence of pure simplicity. It should be modest in size and proportion, in keeping with the property," Jon and I told the architect. At the time, the three of us, all friends for many years, were sitting in the library at 77 Main Street. Jon and I were living there while converting our two-bedroom cottage into a studio and office space and adding what would become the new house.

Located on the corner of two of Nantucket's most beautiful historic streets, Union, lined with its grand, two-hundred-year-old houses, and picturesque Flora, the cottage was plain and uninteresting. The best thing about it was the location, just a block from the center of town. But it was the private patio in the back that attracted us to the cottage. In this sun-filled oasis surrounded by a vine-laden stone wall, one feels that a perfect world really does exist.

Living and working in the same place has always appealed to us. Since Jon and I work together, we create studio/office space wherever we live.

The success of our house depended on consulting with the right architect. We chose C. William Rich, Jr., then a partner in the island firm of Design Associates, because the three of us share an attitude about design. Bill has always lived on and around boats and we liked the way he designed efficient living spaces. We also liked the work he had done with Walter Bienecke, the man responsible for most of the restoration of the island's historic buildings and the Nantucket marina. Because of Bill's long involvement with the island, we knew he would design a house consistent with the architectural style of the historic district. Further, we knew he could create exciting space in a compact house.

The house is open and airy because of the many windows and French doors across its back. The interest comes from the architecture and is not dependent on the furnishings, which are spare. There are level changes rather than walls defining the space, and each level

Left and right: A loftlike bedroom and bath fill the second floor. The room has a spartan quality, wholly unexpected and subtly luxurious. The lace-edged linens are mixed with favorite antique pillowcases from the south of France.

conveys a different feeling.

The entrance is a Mexican-tiled room that leads to a brick patio in the back. To the left and up two steps is the house. To the right is the office with the design studio beyond.

In the house, changes of ceiling height, walls that stop short, a curve in the stairway wall, and the interplay of light from half-seen rooms create elements of surprise. The virtual absence of detailing in this simple scheme is a major factor in its success.

We often use the house to photograph for our books or magazine features. The rose-patterned chintz slipcovers in the living room were made for one such project. The pattern is easy to live with, so we never went back to the white canvas underneath. Lloyd Flanders' old-fashioned wicker chairs are used inside as well as on the deck. The cushions are covered with water-repellent fabric and the furniture is impervious to the weather. Slip-covers in the chintz pattern are

Left: A short hallway off the living room leads one step down into a cozy den. This room was designed to have the cocoonlike quality of a boat cabin. There's a corner fireplace and everything is built-in.

Bottom left: The open kitchen at the front of the house is separated from the living room by an island counter. Pull-up stools make it easy to prepare food and socialize at the same time. Entertaining is carefree and casual and there is a free flow out to the summer living areas.

Right: You might not notice the three white freesias in a white bowl on a white antique lace cloth against the white wall, but the scent of the flowers perfumes the room. The table and cane chairs were bought at a local auction.

used when the furniture comes indoors.

"We need a cozy winter room," we told Bill when we were designing the house. And that's exactly what we got. There's a corner fireplace and a hearth made of small, irregular bricks. Everything is built-in, the windows are high, and it's as intimate as the cabin of a boat. Seating runs around two walls. Shelves wrap around the room to hold books, collectibles, and family photographs. The television, stereo, and VCR fit neatly in a floor-to-ceiling, ready-to-finish armoire that we stained to look old. We've created most of the furnishings, accessories, and craft objects in the house. The rest was bought at auction.

Nantucket is more than a summer resort to us. It has been our home for many years and we are totally seduced by this island. It's absolutely intrinsic to our lives. Each time we head for the airport we are reminded that there are only two kinds of people who leave Nantucket: those who will return, and those who wish they could.

FENCES

Fences are an essential part of the image of Nantucket. While there are many fence styles, pickets prevail. The most elegant fences in town were built by ship's carpenters. Influenced by ship design, the characteristic fence form is wooden with a top rail. Fences create a continuous edge along the street, linking the houses. There are two acceptable paint colors: grey and white. Many fences, left unpainted, turn a soft, silvery grey in the salt air.

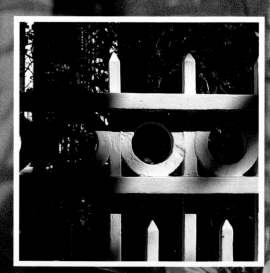

SOURCES

Nantucket Island is known for many things: seemingly endless stretches of shoreline, an unexcelled harbor, an abundance of fine dining establishments, the variety of its downtown shops, art galleries along the wharf, handmade crafts, and charming inns. When planning a visit to Nantucket, it is recommended that you contact the Nantucket Island Chamber of Commerce. They will be more than happy to send you information about Nantucket's facilities for visitors and can offer up-to-the-minute information regarding events, shop operating hours, and anything else to make a visit more enjoyable. You may write or telephone them at the Pacific Club Building, Nantucket, Massachusetts, 02554, (508) 228-1700.

For the sources listed in this section, please note that all street addresses on Nantucket carry the 02554 zip code and that the area code for all telephone numbers is 508 unless otherwise indicated.

MADE ON NANTUCKET

Art Galleries

Janis Aldrige, Inc.
7 Centre Street
228-6673

Irmgard P. Arvin Studio
Milk Street Extension
228-1659

Roy Bailey Studio-Gallery
82 Union Street
228-6755

James Hunt Barker Galleries
1 Pleasant Street
228-0878

Capizzo and Mielko Gallery
Straight Wharf
228-9028

George P. Davis at the Granary
Old South Wharf
228-9525

Expressions of Don Freedman
Old South Wharf
228-3291

G.S. Hill Gallery
Old South Wharf
228-4282

Gallery 1
1 Candle Street
228-2096

Gallery North
Old North Wharf
228-5619

Sybil Goldsmith Studio
9 West Chester Street
228-9291

Hallam Gallery
Old South Wharf
228-2100

Hoorn-Ashby Gallery and the George Murphy Studio
10 Federal Street
228-9314

Hostetler Gallery
Old South Wharf
228-5152

S. Warren Krebs Studio Gallery
57 Union Street
228-4655

Paul LaPaglia Antique Print Gallery
38 Centre Street
228-8760

Little Gallery
Straight Wharf

John F. Lochtefeld Studio Gallery
4A Fair Street
228-0604

Paul O. Longenecker Studio
24 Union Street
228-9143

Main Street Gallery
50 Main Street
228-4027

Maggie Meredith Studio
1 South Mill Hill Road
228-2359

Mielko Gallery
Old South Wharf
228-0014

Nantucket Gallery and Frame Shop
23 Federal Street
228-1943

Nantucket Print and Poster
30 Main Street
228-6876

One New Street Gallery
Siasconset

C. Robert Perrin Gallery
91 Washington Street Extension
228-4107

Arden Rose Gallery
Old South Wharf

Donn Russell Studio and Gallery
Old South Wharf
228-3931

Sailor's Valentine Gallery
40 Centre Street
228-2011

Saltbox Studio
South Mill Street
228-4302

Sherburne Gallery
48 Main Street
228-6246

South Wharf Gallery
Old South Wharf
228-0406

Spectrum of American Artists
26 Main Street
228-4606

Spindrift Gallery
Old South Wharf
228-5173

Robert W. Stark Gallery
Old North Wharf
228-3809

John Stobart Gallery
Straight Wharf
228-1011

Tonkin of Nantucket
33 Main Street
228-9697

Teryl Townsend Gallery
Old South Wharf
228-9497

George C. Thomas
8 Monomoy Creek Road
228-5303

William H. Welch Gallery
14 Easy Street
P.O. Box 2847 02584
228-0687

Crafts

Gretchen Anderson
Museum Shops
Broad Street
228-5785
Classic reed and twisted-seagrass
baskets

Artisans' Cooperative
58 Main Street
228-3766
Quilts, needlepoint, knitwear

Bee Works
14 South Valley Road
228-9324
Custom knit designs

Nancy Chase
Off Surfside Road
228-0959
Ivory carvings, scrimshaw

Craftmasters of Nantucket
7 India Street
228-0322
Jewelry, scrimshaw, leather goods

The Crafts Centre
4 Quaker Road
228-1572
Ivory and wood carvings

Geo. P. Davis, Inc.
Old South Wharf
228-9525, 228-0167
Ceramics, home accessories

Diana Kim England
Artisans Cooperative
58 Main Street
228-3766
Miniature gold lightship baskets

Fletcher Company
69 Monomoy Road
228-9282
Quarterboards, baskets

Four Winds Craft Quild
Straight Wharf
228-9623
Lightship baskets, scrimshaw

Susan Ferdnald Joyce
Artists' Association of Nantucket
Straight Wharf
228-5228
Quiltmaker

Michael Kane Carvers Guild
18-1/2 Sparks Ave.
228-1548
Lightship baskets, scrimshaw

Michael Kinney
P.O. Box 2079
228-5426
Clockmaker

The Lightship Shop
20 Miacomet Avenue
228-4234

Peter Lochtefeld
Lochtefeld Studio Gallery
4A Fair Street
228-0604
Pottery

The Museum Shops
Broad Street
228-5785
Country gifts, furniture

Nantucket Accent
11 South Water Street
228-1913
Hooked rugs, quilts by Claire Murray

Nantucket Basket Works
14 Dave Street
228-2518
Lightship baskets, scrimshaw

Nantucket Candle Shop
Old South Road
228-1487
Candles

Nantucket Designs for Children
12 Orange Street
228-2997

Smocked dresses for children

Nantucket Lightship Baskets
Old South Wharf
P.O. Box 2429
228-2326

Baskets by Richard and Trisha
Anderson

Nantucket Looms
16 Main Street
228-1908

Woven fabrics, home accessories,
gifts

**Margaret Grandin Nettles
Weaving Studio**
64 Union Street
228-9533

Woven rugs

Karl and Susan Chase Ottison
170 Orange Street
228-9345

Lightship baskets

Lee A. Papale
170 Orange Street
228-9504

Scrimshaw

Reyes Baskets
16 York Street
228-0997

Lightship baskets

Bill and Judy Sayle
Washington Street Extension
228-9876

Lightship baskets

Ram Pasture Weavers
Box 1063
228-0333

Handwoven garments

Straight Wharf Quarterboard Co.
16 Meadow View Drive
228-1863

Stephen Swift
Old Quidnet Milk Route
228-0255

Woodworking, fine furniture

The Weaving Room
73 Orange Street
228-9047

Anna Lynn's woven rugs and clothing

Erica Wilson, Inc.
25 Main Street
228-9881

Needlepoint, hooked rugs, quilts, kits

Food Specialities, Bakeries

The Beach Plum Cafe
9 West Creek Road
228-2519

Baguettes, Portuguese bread,
sweets

Espresso Cafe
40 Main Street
228-6930

Salads, sandwiches, sweets, baked
daily

Fast Forward
117 Orange Street
228-5807

Take-out coffee, a good selection of
specialty items and fresh coffee
beans

Glidden's Island Seafoods
Steamboat Wharf
228-0911

E. J. Harvey's Blueberry Muffin
Lower Pleasant Street
P.O. Box 1797
228-7140

Baked goods, gourmet pizza

Nantucket Bake Shop
79 Orange Street
228-2797

Portuguese bread, 'Sconset sweets,
cakes. mail-order gift packages

Nantucket Fine Chocolates
5 Centre Street
228-5444

Provisions
Straight Wharf
228-3258

Fresh breads, sandwiches, desserts

FOR THE HOME

Antiques

The Forager House Collection
22 Broad Street
228-5977

Americana, folk art, antique accessories, baskets, whirligigs, Nantucket memorabilia

Four Winds Craft Guild & Antiques
Straight Wharf
228-9623

Lightship baskets, fine scrimshaw

Nina Hellman
22 Broad Street
228-4677

Nautical antiques, including ship models, navigation instruments, scrimshaw, whaling items, marine paintings, Nantucket memorabilia, folk art, decorative accessories

Hospital Thrift Shop
17 India Street
228-1125

Bric-a-brac, household odds and ends, an unusual antiques-only room, books, antique clothing

Island Attic Industries
Miacomet Avenue (off Surfside Road)
228-9504

A vast warehouse of used and antique furnishings for the home

Paul La Paglia Antique Print Gallery
38 Centre Street
228-8760

Nantucket memorabilia, whaling items

Val Matino Antiques
31 North Liberty Street
228-2747

Lamps and lanterns a specialty

Petticoat Row
19 Centre Street
228-5900

Antique linens, accessories for the home, unusual gifts, tableware, garden furniture

Frank F. Sylvia, Inc.
Ray's Court
228-2258

Furniture, accessories

The Tiller
Easy Street
228-1287

One of Nantucket's oldest shops, specializing in fine furniture, porcelain, brass, and works of art

Tonkin of Nantucket
33 Main Street
228-9697

Furniture, paintings, marine and scientific instruments, silver, English antiques

Tranquil Corners
Sanford Boat Building
49 Sparks Avenue
228-6000

Furniture, accessories, a fine collection of quilts

Vis-a-Vis
34 Main Street
228-5527

Antique lace, linens, hooked rugs, quilts, silver, porcelain

Weeds
14 Centre Street
228-5200

Accessories, furniture

Lynda Willauer Antiques
2 India Street
228-3631

Americana, country accessories, quilts

Gifts & Tabletop

Coffin's Gift Shop
51 Main Street
228-4662

Greeting cards, wrapping paper, country accessories

Crabtree & Evelyn
Centre Street
228-0062

Potpourri, bath luxuries

George P. Davis, Inc. at the Granary
Old South Wharf
228-9525

Home accessories, furniture, lightship baskets

Four Winds Gifts
Straight Wharf
228-1597

Keepsakes, T-shirts

Hill's of Nantucket
Straight Wharf

Holiday ornaments, cards, keepsakes

The Hub of Nantucket
29 Main Street
228-4187

Country accessories

The Lion's Paw
Zero Main Street
228-3837

Tabletop items, bed linens, furniture

The Museum Shop
Broad Street
228-5785

Country accessories, ornaments, furniture, candles, books, toys

Nantucket Looms
16 Main Street
228-1908

Handwoven fabrics, handcrafted gifts and accessories

The Seven Seas Gifts
46 Centre Street
228-0958

Souvenirs, shells, cards

Florists

Bartlett's Ocean View Farm
Bartlett's Farm Road
228-9403

Cut flowers, indoor and outdoor plants

Flowers at The Boarding House
12 Federal Street
228-6007

Unusual plants, creative floral arrangements, country baskets

The Flower Shop at Marine Home Center
Lower Orange Street
228-9008

Cut flowers, indoor and outdoor plants

Grass Roots Bloomists
Zero Washington Street
228-4450

Creative floral arrangements, cut flowers, plants

Mt. Vernon Flowers and Plants
Hummock Pond Road
228-5608

Cut flowers, indoor and outdoor plants

SHOPPING

Booksellers

Mitchell's Book Corner
54 Main Street
228-1080

An entire room is devoted to Nantucket subjects

Nantucket Bookworks
25 Broad Street
228-4000

A fine selection of books, cards, small gifts

Clothing

DeDe Banks
27 Easy Street
228-6633

Beautiful People
13 Centre Street
228-2001

The Bowler Company
12 Main Street
228-9644

Gumballs
P.O. Box 1052
Blueberry Lane
228-1718

Indian Summer Sports
6 Broad Street
228-3632

Irresistibles
34 Main Street
228-9280

Island Pursuit
Straight Wharf
228-5117

Island Studios
6 South Water Street
228-3356

Kado Clothes
Easy Street
228-3270

Marie Claire
7 South Beach Street
228-2089

The Marina Clothing Company
5 Old South Wharf
228-6868

Miss Wear
3 Old South Wharf
228-1241

Murray's Toggery Shop
62—68 Main Street
228-0437

Home of "Nantucket Reds"

Murray's Warehouse
7 New Street
228-3584

For great bargains

Nantucket Designs for Children
12 Orange Street
228-2997

Nantucket Mills
1 North Beach Street
228-1277

Nantucket Model T's
22 Centre Street
228-4600

Nantucket Off Shore
Straight Wharf
228-5529

Nantucket Sportslocker
30 Main Street
228-5669

Nobby Clothes Shop
17 Main Street
228-1030

Pinwheels
5 South Beach Street
228-1238

Children's clothing

Janet Russo
28 Main Street
228-4818

South Side Fashions
62 Old South Road
228-1408

T-Shirt Shop
Straight Wharf
The Courtyard

Together
19 Main Street
228-3181

Top Drawer
8 India Street
228-5556

Upper Deck
34 Main Street
228-7088

Upstairs Downstairs
21 Main Street
228-4250

Vanity Fair Boutique
34 Main Street
228-5527, 228-9102

Joan Vass
23 Centre Street
228-7118

WD and Company
9 Centre Street
228-6734

Wildflowers
The Nantucket Commons
4 Bayberry Court
228-8724

Windjammer Clothing Company
Straight Wharf
228-5136

Winslow's
57A Old South Road
228-1013

Yolanda's
1 North Beach Street
228-0024

Zero Main Street
Zero Main Street
228-4401

Drugstores, Pharmacies

Congdon's Pharmacy
47 Main Street
228-0020

Island Pharmacy
Finast Plaza
Sparks Avenue
228-6400

Nantucket Pharmacy
45 Main Street
228-0180

Jewelry

Avanti
4 Federal Street
228-5833

Antique jewelry

Earrings, Etc.
29 Centre Street
228-9530

The Golden Basket
44 Main Street
228-9530

Miniature 14K gold Nantucket
lightship baskets, original designs

The Golden Nugget
Straight Wharf
228-1019

Jewel of the Isle
35 Old South Road
228-2448

Fine jewelry, custom designs,
watches

Nancy Kenney of Nantucket
18A Federal Street
228-1341

The Jeweler's Gallery
21 Centre Street
228-0229

Gold and sterling silver, precious
stones, estate jewelry

Patina
Old South Wharf
228-6154

S.J. Patten
35 Main Street
228-4882
Fine jewelry, original designs

Tranquil Corners Antiques
Sanford Boat Building
Sparks Avenue
228-6000
Antique jewelry at reasonable prices

SERVICES

Barstow Architects
5 Barstow Lane
228-8457

Bill Bevers
8 Tawpoot Road
228-5246
Upholstery, curtains, drapes, pillows

Brian's Carpets
P.O. Box 1255
228-2626
Custom carpeting

Chin's
Miacomet Avenue
228-4300
Catering

Claudette's Catering
10 Main Street
P.O. Drawer 24
Siasconset, MA 02564
257-6622
Catering

Cynthia Collins
Madaket
228-4966
Landscape and garden design

George Davis and Bruce Dilts
Granary Gallery
Old South Wharf
228-9525
Interior design

Design Associates
58 Main Street
228-4342
Architecture

Dias Landscaping, Inc.
P.O. Box 1826
228-3091
Garden and landscape design

Fabric Workshop
Bruce Thibodeau
6 Salros Road
228-9525
Upholstery, draperies, pillows

Nicholas Ferrantella
P.O. Box 1357
228-4497
Gardening, landscape design

Susan Fisher Catering
12 Somerset Lane
P.O. Box 2103
02584
228-5776
Catering

Flyaway Fare
15 South Beach Street
228-1394
Catering

Furniture n' Things
11 Nancy Ann Lane
228-3172
Ready-to-finish furniture, custom
furniture, and finishing

Timothy Grutzius Design
P.O. Box 1350
228-2289
Garden and landscape design

E.J. Harvey's
Lower Pleasant Street
228-6789
Catering

Christopher F. Holland
8 Williams Lane
228-6968
Architecture

Pamela Humphries
16 Pilgrim Road
228-1312
Contract painting, faux finishes

Island Restoration
Madaket Road
228-2999
Furniture restoration, decorative
finishes

Gary Knight Ltd.
Hummock Pond
228-2571

Interior decoration

The Landscape Company
8 Priscilla Lane
228-1755

Garden and landscape design

Frank Marks Landscaping
44 Hooper Farm Road
228-2094

Garden and landscape design

G.E. Maskell Landscaping
P.O. Box 1455
228-4675

Garden and landscape design

Nantucket Clambake Company
72 Skyline Drive
228-9283

Clambake catering

Nantucket Design Center
13 Old South Road
228-9207

Interior design

Nantucket Interiors
33 North Liberty Street
228-3365

Interior design

Nantucket Picnic Basket
7 North Beach Street
228-5177

Catering, beach lunches

Nantucket Sewing Center
1 Federal Street
P.O. Box 99
228-3846

Custom sewing, tailoring

One Room At A Time
P.O. Box 3145
228-5581

Interior design

Que Sera Sarah
15 South Beach Street
228-1395

Catering, cooking classes

Milton Rowland & Associates
4 Bartlett Road
228-2044

Architecture

Julie Sanford Interiors
19 Lily Street
228-4309

Interior design

'Sconset Gardener
97 Hummock Pond Road
228-3422

Garden and landscape design

Gail Sharretts
16 Federal Street
228-9843

Faux finishes, murals

Short & Ford Architects
35 Quidnet Road
228-2644

Architecture

Take Five
5 Mill Street
228-0254

Cooking classes

Threads Inc.
117 Pleasant Street
228-4561

Tailoring, custom sewing, upholstery

Jeanette D. Topham
Hummock Pond Road
228-1792

Catering

Valero & Sons, Inc.
60 Old South Road
228-2397

Garden and landscape design

Vincent's
21 South Water Street
228-0189

Catering

Lucinda Young
Young's Way
228-5188

Garden and landscape design

ACTIVITIES

Cultural Organizations

The Artists' Association of Nantucket
35 Old South Road
P.O. Box 1104
228-5316

Maria Mitchell Association
2 Vestal Street
228-9198
Astronomy, natural sciences

Nantucket Arts Council
P.O. Box 554
228-2227

Nantucket Atheneum
Lower India Street
P.O. Box 808
228-1110
Library

Nantucket Chamber Music Center
4 Winter Street
228-3352

Nantucket Historical Association
2 Union Street
P.O. Box 1016
228-1894

Nantucket Lifesaving Museum
Polpis Road
P.O. Box L
228-1885

Nantucket Musical Arts Society
P.O. Box 897
228-3735

**Nantucket Island School of Design
and the Arts**
Wauwinet Road
P.O. Box 1848
228-9248

Noonday Concerts
11 Orange Street
(Unitarian Church)
P.O. Box 1023
228-0738

Entertainment

Actor's Theatre of Nantucket
17 Helen's Drive
228-6325
Write for season's schedule

The Box
16 Dave Street
P.O. Box 2122
228-2518
Live music, dancing

Brotherhood of Thieves
23 Broad Street
Live music

**The Club Car
with Scott Olsen**
1 Main Street
228-1101
Piano bar

Dreamland Theatre
19 South Water Street
228-5356
Movies

Gaslight Theatre
North Union Street
228-4435
Movies

**The Harbor House
with Phil & Elizabeth**
P.O. Box 3196
228-1500
228-9138
Music, dancing

Jared's
Jared Coffin House
Broad Street
228-2405
Piano music

The Muse
Surfside Road
228-9716
Live music and dancing

Rose and Crown
23 South Water Street
228-2595
Live music and dancing

'Sconset Casino
New Street
Siasconset, 02564
Movies in season

Siasconset Casino Association
9 Coffin Road
Siasconset, 02564
On-stage play performances in
season

Slide Show
(Methodist Church Performance
Center)
Federal Street
228-3783
Slides of Nantucket shown nightly

The Summer House
Ocean Avenue
Siasconset, 02564
257-9976
Piano music, dancing

The Tap Room
Jared Coffin House
Broad Street
Piano music

Theatre Workshop
P.O. Box 1297
228-0195
Live play performances nightly in
season

Vincent's
21 South Water Street
228-0189
Live music

The Whale
89 Easton Street
228-0313
Live music

The White Elephant
55 Easton Street
228-5500
Live music

Windsong Seafood Bar and Grill
27 Macy Lane
228-6900
Live music

Historic Buildings, Museums, and Points of Interest

For current information about hours and entrance fees at houses and museums, inquire at the Nantucket Historical Association office, 2 Union Street, or call 228-1894.

1800 House
4 Mill Street

Cranberry Bog
Open during October harvest season

Fair Street Museum and Quaker Meeting House
Fair Street

Great Point Lighthouse
Great Point
Access by four-wheel-drive vehicles only

Greater Light
Howard Street
Between Gardner and Main

Hadwen House
96 Main Street
Built in 1845

Hinchman House
7 Milk Street

Loines Observatory
Milk Street Extension

Thomas Macy Warehouse
Straight Wharf

Maria Mitchell Aquarium
29 Washington Street

Maria Mitchell Science Center
2 Vestal Street

The Maria Mitchell House
1 Vestal Street

Old Gaol (1805)
15 Vestal Street

Old Mill (1746)
Prospect & South Mill Street

Old North Church Tower
62 Centre Street

Oldest House
Sunset Lane
Built in 1686

Sankaty Lighthouse
Siasconset Bluff

South Church
Orange Street

Tours

Barrett's Island Tours
20 Federal Street
228-0174

Nantucket Whaling Museum
Broad Street
Daily guided tours, 11 a.m.–3 p.m.

First Congregational Church Tower Tours
Centre Street
228-0950
Climb the church tower for the best scenic view of Nantucket.
Open June–September, 10 a.m.–4 p.m.

Unitarian Church (South Church)
Orange Street
228-2730
Church open for viewing of mid-nineteenth-century trompe l'oeil interior. Listed in the National Register of Historic Places

Quaker Houses Cobbled Lanes
257-6662
A walking tour of historic Nantucket conducted by author and photographer Dick Mackay

Historic Walking Tours
228-1062
A walking tour of historic Nantucket streets sponsored by the Nantucket Historical Association and conducted by a native Nantucketer, Roger Young. Informative, casual, and lots of fun

SPORTS

Bicycle Rentals

Cook's Cycles
6 South Beach Street
228-0800

Holiday Cycle
4 Chester Street
228-3644

Island Cycle
Straight Wharf
228-9224

Nantucket Bike Shop
Steamboat Wharf
228-1999

Young's Bicycle Shop
Steamboat Wharf
228-1151

Boat Charters

***Albacore* fishing charter**
Straight Wharf-Slip 17
228-1439
Three trips per day

Beach Excursions, Ltd. Surf Fishing
One Old North Wharf
228-3728
Equipment provided for surf fishing

***Endeavor* sloop**
Straight Wharf
228-5585

***Flicka* fishing charter**
Straight Wharf-Slip 16
228-9224

Harbor Cruises
Straight Wharf
228-1444
Café and boat rides

Harbor Sail Livery
Washington Street Extension
228-1757
Sailboats for rent

Herbert T
Straight Wharf
228-5622
Fishing charter

Indian Summer Sports
6 Steamboat Wharf
Lower Orange Street
228-3632
Windsurfers

Island Windsurfing
118 Orange Street
228-9401
Windsurfers

Just Do It
Straight Wharf
228-5585
Fishing charter

Little Richard's
Jetties Beach
228-9401
Windsurfers and Hobie Cats

Whitney Mitchell
15 Masaquet Avenue
228-2331
Surf fishing

Moonshadow
Straight Wharf
228-1512
Sport-fishing charters

Nantucket Sail Inc.
Commercial Wharf
228-4897
Sail and outboards rental

Nantucket Whale Watch
Straight Wharf
228-6778
800-322-0013

Sea Tabby
228-1333
Motor yacht rental

Tennis

Jetties Beach Tennis Courts
North Beach Street
228-3028
Open to public, changing room

Miacomet Tennis Courts
Sommerset Road
228-4546
Open to public, no facilities

Nantucket Racquet Club
10 Young's Way
228-0155
Squash, racquet ball, public

The Nantucket Tennis Club

Westmoor Lane off Cliff Road

228-3611

Clay courts, open to public, seasonal and guest memberships available, pro shop, racquet rentals, instruction

Seacliff Tennis Club

North Beach Street

228-0030

Open to public, daily, monthly, seasonal rates, instruction, lounge, racquet rentals

Tristram's Landing Tennis Center

440 Arkansas Avenue

Madaket

228-4588

Private

Golf Courses

Miacomet Golf Club

off Somerset Road

228-9764

Open to the public

Sankaty Head Golf Club

Sankaty Road

257-6391

Private

Siasconset Golf Club

Milestone Road

257-6596

Open to the public

Health Club

Nantucket Health and Fitness

45 Surfside Road

228-3945

TRANSPORTATION

Airlines/Scheduled

Business Express

Bridgeport/Sikorsky Airport

Stratford, CT 06497

800-345-3400

The Delta Connection serving Boston and New York

Eastern Express

Nantucket Memorial Airport

800-EASTERN or 228-3672

Express Air

Nantucket Memorial Airport

800-852-2332

Serving New Bedford and the islands, charter flights available

Nantucket Airlines

Nantucket Memorial Airport

228-6234

800-635-8787—Mass. only

Serving Nantucket and Hyannis, charter flights available

Spectrum Airlines

Nantucket Memorial Airport

800-332-2515

Serving New Bedford and Nantucket

Tri-Air

Barnstable Municipal Airport

Hyannis, MA 02601

771-4888

Hourly commuter flights between New Bedford and Nantucket

Airlines/Charters

Cape Cod Air

Municipal Airport

Chatham, MA 02633

800-553-2376 (Mass. only)

Coastal Air Services

Groton-New London Airport

Groton, CT 06040

203-448-1001 or 228-3350

Rainbow Air, Inc.

Princeton-Nantucket

609-921-3867

Ferries

Bay State Cruises

20 Long Wharf

Boston, MA 02110

617-723-7800

Service from Boston from May to October, one round-trip daily, passengers/bicycles only, no cars

Hy-Line

Pier 1 Ocean Street Dock

Hyannis, MA 02601

508-775-7187

Service from Hyannis from May to October for passengers and bicycles, no cars

Woods Hole, Martha's Vineyard, Nantucket Steamship Authority

P.O. Box 284 Dept. NC

Woods Hole, MA 02543

508-540-2022

Daily trips year-round from South Street Dock, Hyannis. Car reservations must be made in advance.

Nantucket Boat Basin

Nantucket has a full-service marina. Reservations must be made well in advance by calling the Dockmaster at:

Nantucket Boat Basin
228-1333

Fees are charged by location of mooring and size of boat.

ACCOMMODATIONS

Apartments

95 Orange Street Apartment
95 Orange Street
228-6597

Anchor Inn
66 Centre Street
P.O. Box 387
228-0072

Bed 'n' Breakfast on Nantucket
22 Lovers Lane
228-9040

Brant Point Inn
6 North Beach Street
228-5442

Calvin Lombard House
72 Union Street
228-4252

The Centerboard
8 Chester Street
P.O. Box 456
228-9696

Cliffside Beach Apartments
Jefferson Avenue
P.O. Box 449
228-0618

Eighteen Gardner Street Apartments
18 Gardner Street
228-1155

Fair Winds
29 Cliff Road
228-1998

The Grey Goose Apartments
24 Hussey Street
P.O. Box 1337
228-6597

The Grey Lady
34 Centre Street
P.O. Box 1292
228-9552

La Petite Maison
132 Main Street
228-9242

Nantucket Breeze
133 Old South Road
228-4889

Nantucket Whaler Apartments
8 North Water Street
P.O. Box 1337
228-6597

Salted Down
off Hummock Pond Road
228-2601

Silver Falls
4-1/2 Silver Street
228-2104

Six Ash Lane
6 Ash Lane
P.O. Box 426
228-4133

Still Dock Apartments
Still Dock
c/o 9 Cliff Road
228-9480

Wade Housekeeping Apartments
Shell Street
P.O. Box 211
Siasconset, MA 02564
257-6308

Bed and Breakfast

The 1739 House
43 Centre Street
P.O. Box 997
228-0120

31 Pleasant Street
31 Pleasant Street
228-0673

40 West Chester Street
40 West Chester Street
228-2740

55 Fair Street
55 Fair Street
228-2027

76 Main Street
76 Main Street
228-2533

Anchor Inn
66 Centre Street
P.O. Box 387
228-0072

Atlantic Mainstay
8 North Beach Street
228-5451

The Beachway Guest House
3 North Beach Street
228-1324

Bed 'n' Breakfast on Nantucket
22 Lovers Lane
228-9040

Brant Point Inn
6 North Beach Street
228-5442

The Brass Lantern
11 North Water Street
228-4064

Carlisle House
26 North Water Street
228-0720

The Carriage House
5 Ray's Court
228-0326

The Centerboard
8 Chester Street
P.O. Box 456
228-9696

Century House
10 Cliff Road
P.O. Box 603
228-0530

Claire's B&B
90 Skyline Drive
P.O. Box 3294
228-8966

Cliff House
34 Cliff Road
228-2154

Cliff Lodge
9 Cliff Road
228-9480

Cobblestone Inn
5 Ash Street
228-1987

Corner House
49 Centre Street
P.O. Box 1828
228-1530

Danforth House
121 Main Street
228-0136

Dolphin Guest House
10 North Beach Street
228-4028

Easton House
17 North Water Street
P.O. Box 1033
228-2759

Eighteen Gardner Street Inn
18 Gardner Street
228-1155

Fair Gardens
27 Fair Street
228-4258

Fair Winds
29 Cliff Road
228-1998

The Fairway
9 Fair Street
228-9467

Four Ash Street
4 Ash Street
P.O. Box 765
228-4899

The Four Chimneys
38 Orange Street
228-1912

Great Harbor Inn
31 India Street
228-6609

House of the Seven Gables
32 Cliff Road
228-4706

House of York
17 York Street
228-3485

The Hungry Whale
8 Derrymore Road
228-0793

Hussey House
15 North Water Street
P.O. Box 552
228-0747

La Petite Maison
132 Main Street
228-9242

Martin's Guest House
61 Centre Street
P.O. Box 743
228-0678

Nantucket Landfall
4 Harbor View Way
228-0500

One Cottage Court
1 Cottage Court
P.O. Box 482
228-2486

The Periwinkle
7–9 North Water Street
P.O. Box 1436
228-9267

Phillips House
54 Fair Street
228-9217

Reuben Joy Homestead
107 Main Street
228-1703

Safe Harbor Guest House
2 Harbor View Way
228-3222

Seven Sea Street
7 Sea Street
228-3577

The Stumble Inne
109 Orange Street
228-4482

Ten Hussey Street
10 Hussey Street
P.O. Box 1292
228-9552

Ten Lyon Street
10 Lyon Street
228-5040

Tuckernuck Inn
60 Union Street
228-4886

Union Street Inn
7 Union Street
228-9222

Lynda Watts Guest House
10 Upper Vestal Street
228-2950

Cottages and Houses

Amoor Cottage on Long Pond
Massasoit Village
228-6548

Atlantic Avenue Cottage
78 Orange Street
228-9364

Aurora Cottage
34 Walsh Street
(813) 566-8275

Back-A-Bit Cottage
13101 D'Artagnan
St. Louis, MO 63141
228-2623

Bartlett's Beach Cottages
Hummock Pond Road
P.O. Box 899
228-9403

Boathouse Cottage
Old North Wharf
228-9552

Brush Cottages
5 Grove Lane
228-6597

Cabot Lane Cottages
2 Cabot Lane
228-2377

Capizzo Cottages
P.O. Box 225
228-2237

Chestnut House
3 Chestnut Street
228-0049

Christman Cottages
Washington Street
P.O. Box 1447
228-1290

Cliffside Beach Cottages
Jefferson Avenue
P.O. Box 449
228-0618

Corkish Cottages
Polpis Road
228-1828

Craig Cottage
Brant Point
P.O. Box 689
228-0258

Crow's Nest Associates
38 Wauwinet Road
228-5512

Diana Cottage
34 Walsh Street
c/o Aurora Cottage
(813) 566-8275

The Dinghy in Sconset
10 Cliff Road
228-0530

Dionis Beach Cottages
P.O. Box 247
228-4524

Escape Hatch at Surfside
Surfside
c/o Aurora Cottage
(215) 357-2786

Far Island Farm
43 Madaket Road
228-4227

The Folger Cottages
Easton Street
P.O. Box 628
228-0313

Grieder Waterfront Cottages
Madaket
P.O. Box 333
228-1399

Halliday's Cottage
2 East York Street
P.O. Box 165
228-9450

Harbor Front Cottage
56 Washington Street
(617) 334-4731

Holdgate's Cottages
Washington Street
P.O. Box 146
228-2475

Horatio at Brant Point
34 Walsh Street
c/o Aurora Cottage
(813) 566-8275

Le Cottage
1A Fayette Street
228-3850

Lowell Cottages
Main Street at New Lane
P.O. Box 1054
228-1182

Monomoy Village
4 Federal Street
P.O. Box 776
228-4449

The Mute Swan
8 Brooks Road
Rockport, MA 01966
(508) 546-7395

Old North Wharf
P.O. Box 2340, 02584
228-6071

R&R Vacation Homes
P.O. Box 2227, 02584
228-2948

Stone Alley Cottage
Stone Alley
P.O. Box 1182
228-9529

Summer House
Ocean Avenue
P.O. Box 313
Siasconset, MA 02564
257-9976

Sunny Acres Cottage
61 Surfside Road
228-0986

Taylor Cottages
152 Main Street
P.O. Box 624
228-0519

Toombs Cottages
9 Toombs Court
P.O. Box 803
228-0157

Tristram's Landing
Madaket
228-0359

Wade Cottages
Shell Street
P.O. Box 211
Siasconset, MA 02564
257-6308

Westmoor Cottages
off Cliff Road
P.O. Box 1811
228-6561

Wharf Cottages
Swain's Wharf
P.O. Box 1139
228-5500

White Elephant Cottages
Easton Street
P.O. Box 359
228-5500

Guest Houses

3 Hussey Street
3 Hussey Street
P.O. Box 1829
228-4298

Ayers House
6 Union Street
P.O. Box 1087
228-0245

Chestnut House
3 Chestnut Street
228-0049

Cranberry Guest House
33 Centre Street
P.O. Box 1267
228-2821

Fair Winds
29 Cliff Road
228-1998

The Grey Lady
34 Centre Street
P.O. Box 1292
228-9552

Grieder Guest House
43 Orange Street
P.O. Box 333
228-1399

Halliday's Nantucket House
2 East York Street
P.O. Box 165
228-9450

The Hawthorn House
2 Chestnut Street
228-1468

The House at Ten Gay Street
10 Gay Street
228-4425

The House of Orange
25 Orange Street
228-9287

The Island Reef
20 North Water Street
P.O. Box 1267
228-2156

Ivy Lodge
2 Chester Street
228-0305

Main Street At New Lane
Main Street at New Lane
P.O. Box 1054
228-1182

Nesbitt Inn
21 Broad Street
P.O. Box 1019
228-0156

Parker Guest House
4 East Chestnut Street
228-4625

Sixfair
6 Fair Street
228-0679

Star of the Sea Hostel
Surfside
228-0433

Wade Guest House
Shell Street
P.O. Box 211
Siasconset, MA 02564
257-6308

Walker Guest House
5 Fair Street
228-0213

Paul West House
5 Liberty Street
P.O. Box 214
228-2495

While-Away Guest House
4 Gay Street
P.O. Box 64
228-1102

Hotels—Motels—Inns

Anchor Inn
66 Centre Street
P.O. Box 387
228-0072

The Barnacle Inn
11 Fair Street
P.O. Box 817
228-0332

Beachside Resort at Nantucket
North Beach Street
228-2241

The Carriage House
5 Ray's Court
228-0326

Cliffside Beach Club
Jefferson Avenue
P.O. Box 449
228-0618

Corner House
49 Centre Street
P.O. Box 1828
228-1530

The Folger Hotel
Easton Street
P.O. Box 628
228-0313

Harbor House
South Beach Street
P.O. Box 1048
228-5500

Holiday Inn
78 Centre Street
228-0199

Small guest house—not part of a chain

India House
37 India Street
P.O. Box 576
228-9043

Jared Coffin House
29 Broad Street
P.O. Box J
228-2405

Le Languedoc
24 Broad Street
P.O. Box 1829
228-4298

Manor House Inn
31 Centre Street
P.O. Box 1436
228-5551

Nantucket Inn at Nobadeer
Macy Lane
228-6900

Nesbitt Inn
21 Broad Street
P.O. Box 1019
228-0156

The Overlook Hotel
3 Step Lane
P.O. Box 1112
228-0695

Quaker House Inn
5 Chestnut Street
228-0400

Roberts House
11 India Street
P.O. Box 1436
228-9009

Seven Sea Street
7 Sea Street
228-3577

Ships Inn
13 Fair Street
228-0040

The Summer House
Ocean Avenue
P.O. Box 313
Siasconset, MA 02564
257-9976

The Wauwinet
Wauwinet Road
P.O. Box 2580
228-0145

Westmoor Inn
off Cliff Road
228-4008

The White Elephant
Easton Street
P.O. Box 359
228-5500

The Woodbox Inn
29 Fair Street
228-0587

Interval Ownership

Tristram's Landing
Madaket
228-0359

Reservation Services

Heaven Can Wait
P.O. Box 622
257-4000

Nantucket Accomodations
P.O. Box 217
228-9559

DINING

Casual Restaurants

Arno's Seafood
41 Main Street
228-5857

The Atlantic Cafe
South Water Street
228-0570

The Beach Plum Cafe
9 West Creek Road
228-2519

The Brotherhood
23 Broad Street

Cap'n Tobey's
Straight Wharf
228-0836

Chin's
Chin's Way
P.O. Box 653
228-0200

The Dory
10 India Street
P.O. Box 566

The Downyflake
South Water Street
228-4533

Elegant Dump
56 Union Street
P.O. Box 688
228-4634

E.J. Harvey's
Lower Pleasant Street
P.O. Box 3146
228-6789

Hutch's at Jetties Beach
P.O. Box 701
228-5818

The Tap Room at Jared Coffin House
29 Broad Street
P.O. Box J
228-2400

La Vie En Rose
Nantucket Commons
P.O. Box 2489, 02584
228-8743

North Wharf Fish House
12 Cambridge Street
228-5213

Off Centre Cafe
29 Centre Street
P.O. Box 511
228-8470

Quaker House
5 Chestnut Street
228-9156

Rose and Crown
23 South Water Street
P.O. Box D
228-2595

Saratoga Steaks
off Old South Road
228-6346

Sconset Cafe
Post Office Square
P.O. Box 19
Siasconset, MA 02564
257-4008

The Tavern
Harbor Square
P.O. Box 388
228-1266

Vincent's Restaurant
21 South Water Street
228-0189

The Westender
Madaket Road
228-5197

White Dog Cafe
North Union Street
228-4479

Reservations Suggested

American Seasons
80 Centre Street
228-7111

21 Federal Street
21 Federal Street
228-2121

The Boarding House
12 Federal Street
228-9622

Company of the Cauldron
7 India Street
228-4016

The Chanticleer
9 New Street
P.O. Box 601
Siasconset, MA 02564
257-6231

The Club Car
1 Main Street
P.O. Box 1852
228-1101

De Marco
9 India Street
228-1836

The Whale at the Folger Hotel
Easton Street
P.O. Box 628
228-0313

The Galley on Cliffside Beach
Jefferson Avenue
P.O. Box 449-N
228-9641

The Hearth at the Harbor House
South Beach Street
P.O. Box 1048
228-1500

India House
37 India Street
P.O. Box 576
228-9043

Jared's at Jared Coffin House
29 Broad Street
P.O. Box J
228-2400

Le Languedoc
24 Broad Street
P.O. Box 1829
228-2552

Windsong at Nantucket Inn
Macy Lane
228-6900

The Second Story
1 South Beach Street
228-3471

Captain's Table at Ships Inn
13 Fair Street
228-0040

Straight Wharf
Harbor Square
228-4499

Summer House
Ocean Avenue
P.O. Box 313
Siasconset, MA 02564
257-9976

Topper's at the Wauwinet
Wauwinet Road
P.O. Box 2580, 02584
228-8768

The Regatta at White Elephant
Easton Street
P.O. Box 359
228-2500

The Second Story
1 Beach Street
228-3471

The Woodbox
29 Fair Street
228-0587

Sandwiches & Snacks

5 Corners
49A Pleasant Street
228-1546

Claudette's Box Lunches
10 Main Street
Siasconset, MA 02564
257-6622

David's Soda Fountain
47 Main Street
228-4549

The Deli
9 South Water Street
228-3626

Espresso Cafe
40 Main Street
228-6930

Fast Forward
117 Orange Street
228-5807

Foood For Here and There
149 Orange Street
228-4291

E.J. Harvey's Blueberry Muffin
Lower Pleasant Street
228-7140

Henry's Sandwiches
Steamboat Wharf
228-0123

Nantucket Picnic Basket
7 North Beach Street
228-5177

Something Natural
50 Cliff Road
228-0504

Vincent's
21 South Water Street
228-0189

BEACHES

In-Town Beaches

Brant Point
A short bike ride or easy walk from town, overlooks harbor channel, no lifeguard or public facilities

Children's Beach
A short walk from town, calm water, grassy area with playground, lifeguard, snack bar, restrooms

Jetties Beach
The most popular in-town beach, swings and slide, windsurfing, public tennis court, lifeguards, snack bar, restrooms, outdoor showers, picnic tables, umbrella rentals

Out-Of-Town Beaches

Cisco
Rough surf, lifeguard, no public facilities, parking area

Dionis
Calm water, good surf casting, beautiful dunes, three miles from town, lifeguards, no public facilities, served by bike path

Madaket
Five miles from town, served by bike path, lifeguards, no public facilities

Nobadeer
Large beach, no lifeguards or public facilities

Siasconset
Beautiful beach bordering the village of Siasconset, served by bike path, regular bus service from Nantucket town, moderate surf, lifeguards, food service nearby, no restrooms

Surfside
The most popular ocean beach, long shoreline, uncrowded, three miles from town, lifeguards, snack bar, restrooms

NANTUCKET ELSEWHERE

Most of the island's shops and galleries provide mail-order service. If you write or call for information, they will be able to tell you where to find their products off island, if possible. Almost all Nantucket artists and craftspeople are listed with the Artist's Association of Nantucket, and it will provide you with the proper information for contacting artists or galleries directly. The Nantucket style, in furnishings, gifts, artwork, and clothing can be found in many places across the United States and Canada. The sources listed here, by no means complete, are suggestions for those who cannot travel to the island.

Abercrombie & Fitch
1 Limited Parkway
P.O. Box 182168
Columbus, Ohio 43230
614-479-6500

Nautical gifts and clothing. Stores in twenty-six states, phone headquarters for location

America Hurrah Antiques
766 Madison Avenue
New York, NY 10021
212-535-1930

Folk art

Judi Boisson American Antique Quilts
96 Main Street
Southampton, NY 11968
516-283-5466

Charlie's Locker
3410 Via Lido
Newport Beach, CA 92663
714-675-6230

Nautical gifts and clothing

Coast Chandlery
1 Breakwater
Santa Barbara, CA 93109
805-965-4538

Marine supplies, gifts, and clothing

Goldbergs' Marine
12 West 37th Street
New York, NY 10017
212-594-6065

Nautical fashions, fishing gear, boating supplies

Goodspeed's Book Shop, Inc.
7 Beacon Street
Boston, MA 02108
617-523-5970

Marine prints

Old Print Shop
150 Lexington Avenue
New York, NY 10016
212-683-3950

Marine prints

Marine Arts Gallery
135 Essex Street
P.O. Box 816
Salem, MA 01970
508-745-5000

Nineteenth- and twentieth-century oils, watercolors, and drawings of marine subjects

The San Francisco Ship Model Gallery
1089 Madison Avenue
New York, NY 10021
212-570-6767

Ship models

David Schorsch
30 East 76th Street
New York, NY 10021
212-439-6100

Lightship baskets, scrimshaw, furniture

Waverly
79 Madison Avenue
New York, NY 10016
800-423-5881

The Nantucket Collection of fabrics, wallcoverings, and home fashions available in retail stores across the United States. Call or write for information or locations

INDEX

SELECT
BIBLIOGRAPHY

Chamberlin, Barbara Blau. These Fragile Outposts. Garden City, New York: The Natural History Press, 1964.

Duprey, Kenneth. Old Houses on Nantucket. New York: Hastings House, 1984.

Forman, Henry Chandlee. Early Nantucket and its Whale Houses. New York: Hastings House, 1966.

Fowlkes, George Allen. A Mirror of Nantucket. Plainfield, New Jersey: Press of Interstate, 1959.

Hoyt, Edwin P. The Life of an Island. Brattleboro, Vermont: Stephen Greene Press, 1980.

Lancaster, Clay. Nantucket in the Nineteenth Century. New York: Dover Publications, Inc., 1979.

————. The Architectural History of Nantucket. New York: McGraw-Hill, 1972.

Lang, J. Christopher, Building with Nantucket in Mind. Nantucket, Massachusetts: Nantucket Historic District Commission, 1978.

Nantucket Historic District Commission. Nantucket Historic District Guidebook. Nantucket, Massachusetts: The Poet's Corner Press, 1967.

Sterling, Dorothy. The Outer Lands, A Natural History Guide to Cape Cod, Martha's Vineyard, Nantucket, Block Island, and Long Island. New York: W. W. Norton, 1978.

Stevens, William O. Old Nantucket, The Far Away Island. New York: Doss, Mead & Company, 1936.

Turner, Harry Baker. Nantucket Argument Settlers. Nantucket, Massachusetts: The Island Press, 1966.

Whitten, Paul F. Nantucket Baskets. Nantucket, Massachusetts: Paul Whitten, 1988.